UNEXPECTED
MIRACLES IN AN ORDINARY LIFE

True Life Stories of God's Interventions

klay E. ROGERS

Aspire
PUBLISHING
GROUP

CONTENTS

Acknowledgements
Introduction: Celebrating God's Interventions

1 - An Unforgettable Trip 1

2 - What? No Watch? 9

3 - Falsely Accused, Yet Free Indeed! 15

4 - Icy Texas Roads in June! 23

5 - A Specialized Surgery Led by the Hand of God 31

6 - A Cord Repaired 37

7 - We're Twins! 43

8 - Achieving the American Dream! 51

9 - Unexpected Provisions 59

10 - Every Day is a Gift 67

11 - Words of Comfort 75

12 - A Divine Exit and a New Direction 83

13 - Only One Set of Footprints in the Sand? 89

14 - Writing a Musical Comedy 95

15 - A Fiery Furnace that Failed to Ignite 103

16 – What's on Your List? 109

ACKNOWLEDGEMENTS

I'd like to publicly thank a few people for their assistance in the creation of this book. First is my editor, Ms. Melanie Martin of Frisco, Texas. Melanie is a most excellent wordsmith, holds a Masters of Journalism from the University of North Texas, and most importantly has the special ability to take my Texas twang and translate it into something comprehendible to a broad based audience. Melanie has a heart for the Lord and stands ready to help you with your book. You can find her on Facebook or by writing to me.

Secondly, I'd like to thank my cover designer Mr. Bill Wegener of Allen, Texas. With his artistic gift he created the wonderful cover you've already seen and with his gift of photography he made an exceptional portrait of me. Bill loves the Lord and in particular the children of Rwanda. You can also find him and his portfolio of impressive photos on Facebook or by writing to me.

I'd also like to thank my lifelong friend, Sally Sanderson of Circumstance Communications Group for helping me with promotion and bookings. My friend Kelly Brewer has helped by using her keen eye to find those hardest to find errors. Rev. Jerry Wilson of Grace Pointe Community Church in Wylie Texas has provided assistance with finding the many scriptures used in the book. And Ryan Windham has designed the website www.GodsUnexpectedMiracles.com. Again, thank you to you all.

I also want to thank my children, Ashley, Brandon, and Blake for allowing me to follow my heart and sit at the computer for way too long.

Klay Rogers
www.GodsUnexpectedMiracles.com

INTRODUCTION:

CELEBRATING GOD'S INTERVENTIONS

There was a time in the late 1990s when I was driving with my ten-year-old son on a quiet stretch of road between Killeen and Lampasas, Texas when we had a flat tire. I pulled over onto the shoulder to make the change. The sun was on the horizon and darkness was about to settle in. We worked for about 20 minutes when we discovered that we had no tire tool in the car with which to change the tire! My thoughts began to race to find a solution. There was no town, store, or even a farmhouse in sight. Should we start walking? Should we trust a stranger? Would we be stuck on the side of the road all night? This had the potential to be a bad situation. My mind was reeling with the many dangerous scenarios.

Fortunately, within five minutes, a Texas Highway Patrol officer pulled up behind us and offered assistance. The officer knew of a business in Lampasas that was open late that night. So he drove us to this business where the owner gladly gave us a tire tool. The officer then returned us to our car. Under the safety lights of his patrol car we changed the tire and went on our way in record time. Yes, we could have been stranded all night, but the Lord was watching over us. The timing of the flat, the arrival of the patrol officer, and the late-night hours of the business were all a part of God's plan for keeping us safe. To think of how it was resolved was amazing. That night I experienced one of many miracles in my life.

God inhabits the praises of His people. Herein I've documented fifteen true life stories representing times when the Lord has intervened in my life and performed a personal miracle. Some stories describe situations of danger, some depict times of comfort or protection, and others tell how the Lord directed my life in a specific way.

I have two compelling reasons for telling these miraculous stories—first, I am simply grateful to God Almighty for all that he has done for me, and, secondly, I want to share with others *how* God intervenes in our lives. After reading the Old Testament story of King Hezekiah I realized that I am not the only one to feel so grateful. 2 Chronicles 29 and 30 records how King Hezekiah took the throne at age twenty-five and immediately reinstituted worship in the temple which included observance of the great Passover and Feast of the Unleavened Bread. The following events are from 2 Chronicles 30:20-27 and occur after King Hezekiah's lead the people to worship:

And the LORD heard Hezekiah and healed the people.

[21] The Israelites who were present in Jerusalem *celebrated* the Festival of Unleavened Bread for seven days with *great rejoicing*, while the Levites and priests *praised* the LORD every day with resounding instruments dedicated to the LORD.

[22] Hezekiah spoke encouragingly to all the Levites, who showed good understanding of the service of the LORD. For the seven days they ate their assigned portion and *offered fellowship offerings* and *praised the LORD*, the God of their ancestors.

[23] The whole assembly then agreed to _celebrate the festival seven more days_; so for _another seven days_ they _celebrated joyfully_. [24] Hezekiah king of Judah provided a thousand bulls and seven thousand sheep . . . [25] The entire assembly of Judah _rejoiced_, along with the priests and Levites and all who had assembled from Israel, including the foreigners who had come from Israel and also those who resided in Judah. [26] There was _great joy_ in Jerusalem, for since the days of Solomon son of David king of Israel there had been nothing like this in Jerusalem. [27] The priests and the Levites stood to bless the people, and God heard them, for their prayer reached heaven, his holy dwelling place.

(NIV; italics and underscore added for emphasis)

Out of gratitude the people stopped to remember what God had done for them and they observed Passover. Then, the entire assembly celebrated the Feast of the Unleavened Bread—not once, but twice! Verse 23 states that they joyfully celebrated an _additional seven days_. The fullness of their hearts resonated with me and I was stirred by their passion.

Next to this passage in my Bible is a chart summarizing the twelve Old Testament feasts and sacred days. They are celebrations of specific times when God intervened in the lives of the Hebrew people or they represent specific times set aside to honor God for His goodness.

- ❖ The Sabbath
- ❖ The Sabbath Year
- ❖ The Year of Jubilee
- ❖ The Day of Passover

❖ The Feast of the Unleavened Bread
❖ Firstfruits
❖ Weeks (Harvest)
❖ Trumpets (later-Rosh Hashanah)
❖ Day of Atonement (Yom Kippur)
❖ Tabernacles (Booths)
❖ Sacred Assembly
❖ Purim (deliverance in the time of Esther)

After realizing that the Hebrew calendar is filled with celebrations I thought, "I must do the same!" I must be grateful for the personal and unique things that God has done for me. I wish to celebrate personally because the Lord has been as good to me as He was to the Israelites! Thus, this book is my personal festival.

My second reason for these writings is to give testimony of *how* the Lord intervenes in our lives. Sometimes He intervenes upon our request and sometimes He intervenes when we don't recognize His presence. So to those that struggle believing that God cares for people individually, I invite you to consider my stories. I believe in the God of Christianity and that He wants to be involved in our lives if we allow Him.

It is my hope that these stories will help you to understand how God works in your life. I have added questions at the end of each chapter to help you take account of the many ways the Lord has protected, directed and provided for you in your life. May your experience with Him be forever miraculous!

*I will not die, but live and
tell the works of the Lord.*

Psalm 118:17 (NASV)

1

AN UNFORGETTABLE TRIP

In the fall of 1981, I was a 21-year-old student attending the University of Texas in Austin. I am also an avid college football fan. The pageantry, passion, rivalries, and ever changing participants are the best in all of sports.

When I was a child of six my grandparents would invite relatives from Oklahoma to their home in Dallas and we'd all sit religiously in front of the television to watch the Texas vs. Oklahoma football game. This family gathering was an annual ritual, as well as the game between Texas and Oklahoma, which was always played each October during the popular State Fair of Texas. My family cheered for the Longhorns; our Oklahoma kin cheered for the Sooners. That was the time in my young life when I became a loyal Longhorns fan.

I had a friend in Dallas who shared my passion for football. This friend, a licensed pilot, went to all the games because his family had season tickets. One week he called and said he had four tickets to the UT versus Houston Cougars game, which was to be played in the Houston Astrodome. The invitation was for me to join him along with two other friends. The plan was for him to fly to Austin, pick up my two friends and me, fly to Houston, and enjoy the game. Then we'd return to Austin later that night. I was thrilled. It sounded like a great adventure so we made it happen.

Our flight to Houston was uneventful. The weather was beautiful and we enjoyed clear skies and bright sunshine. We arranged for college friends to pick us up at a small local airport and drive us to the game. The Astrodome stood in all its glory that day and was packed to capacity with Longhorns and Cougars fans. For four quarters each team viciously tried to become the better team. The hard-fought game, however, ended in a 14 – 14 tie. That night the score didn't seem to matter so much because we were having a great time. After the game we ate dinner at a nice restaurant, enjoyed each other's company, and headed to the airport for our return flight to Austin.

Everything was going as planned. We settled into the plane, gingerly took off, and headed smoothly to the west. The sky was very dark, thus the stars above us and the ground lights below us glistened like jewels. It was a very peaceful and calm flight, as if we were gliding through the darkness; that is, until unexpectedly all the electronic instruments in the plane suddenly went dark. There was no radio, no navigation equipment, no fuel gauge, nor any other electronic instrument. Suddenly we were all smacked in the face with a stark realization—this was not a good situation. The reality sunk in when the pilot used a flashlight so that he could read the compass on the dashboard. Fortunately, the plane's engine continued to run uninterrupted.

After several moments of thought and some discussion, the pilot determined that it was best for us to return to Houston and land. We wanted to be on the safe side. We'd been airborne for less than thirty minutes and we were still in the Greater Houston area, so to turn around would be an easy answer. I learned something new that night—all airports are marked on the ground by green and white rotating beacons. From the night sky we could see several small airports at which we could land. One airport's runway was outlined in lights. It was already after midnight so we decided that the lit runway was the best choice because landing would be easier and the office may still be open so that we could use the telephone. (This was long before mobile phones were common.) So we began our descent.

My pilot friend was fully trained so a normal landing was routine to him, even at night. But he had limited real-life experience and I could sense that he felt pressured and uncomfortable. What he didn't realize at the moment was that the wing flaps, designed to slow the plane down during landing, also were electronic. His electronic instructions to them were to no avail, so they remained in their up position. This meant that our approach to the runway was going to be much faster than what's typical when wing flaps are engaged.

The plane's headlights also were not operational, so our pilot could not see the approaching ground. Our descent, therefore, was going to occur by "feel." Down we went, expecting the normal touch and soft squeal of the tires. But that did not happen. The plane hit the ground with extreme force and we heard a loud bang as if we were witnessing a bad auto accident. The tires squealed and screeched loudly on the concrete. Then the plane bounced higher than any roller coaster I've ever ridden. Next, there was a second boom and a second bounce. Then a *third!* Finally, the pilot throttled up the engine and the plane lifted into the night sky again.

I looked at my pilot friend and could see that he was visibly shaken. He was sweating. Seriousness covered his face. This wild ride had brought a deafening and tense silence which enveloped all of us. We were silent as well as speechless. The pilot's full attention must remain on this most serious job at hand.

The pilot banked the plane, circled the airport, and prepared to make a second approach. He lined up the plane with the runway, descended in the normal fashion, and once again pounded the ground hard, bouncing several more times. Then, throttle up and we were flying again. My friend certainly had his hands full. (In a later conversation, he said that he could have used a crank to manually lower the wing flaps. This would have helped immensely, but in the pressure of that tense moment, that option didn't come to his mind.)

On the third approach, I spoke to my friend, "Go as slow as you can and come in low." Perhaps my voice and encouraging words made a difference. He changed his approach and landed the plane with less of a bang, applied the brakes, and finally brought the plane to a stop. All four of us breathed a huge sigh of relief as we taxied to the nearest building. The pilot turned off the motor and we exited the plane. Believe me; it was refreshing to finally have our feet on solid ground!

We looked at the plane and saw that the front tire on the landing gear was severely knocked out of alignment. In the coming weeks I learned that the landing gear had to be replaced because of the damage incurred by the hard landing. We never found out why the electronics failed. It didn't really matter because we would never again get back into that plane.

As I walked away from the plane, I looked toward the end of the runway. In that bright starlit night I could see beyond the airport property to a field full of the most beautiful pine trees ever! Pines in Houston grow tall, straight, and frequently reach heights of more than 100 feet. Obviously, there was adequate room for planes to operate safely, however, that doesn't necessarily apply to a plane with no electronics nor wing flaps! I believe it was by the grace of God that our plane did not crash into that wall of pines or have some other tragic result. I wouldn't doubt it if angels were under our wings pushing that plane into flight.

We made a late-night phone call to our college friends and ended up sleeping at their house that night. My pilot friend was so disturbed by the experience that he didn't sleep. Early in the morning, while everyone was still sleeping, he called for a taxi and caught a commercial flight home to Dallas. Later that day, the rest of us returned to Austin riding in the back of a pickup truck with a camper. It wasn't luxurious, but it was safe.

This was the first unexpected miracle in my rather ordinary life.

DISCUSSION QUESTIONS:

1) Does the Lord care about our individual safety? List at least three verses or biblical examples of His promises to protect us.

_____

_____

_____

_____

_____

2) We all know people who have suffered tragic accidents. What reasons might the Lord have for protecting four young men that night?

_____

_____

_____

_____

_____

3) When or how has the Lord protected you from physical injury?

_____

_____

_____

_____

_____

Greater love has no one than this,
that one lay down his life for his friends.

John 15:13 (NASV)

2
WHAT? NO WATCH?

When I was 27 years old I worked as a sales rep for a national publishing company. I was responsible for a territory; thus, I drove around in my truck all day and called on customers. The company published legal material and its customers were law firms and accounting firms. I was required to call into the district office twice a day to check for messages and I'd sometimes go into the office for meetings. But for the most part, I worked from my home office or out of my truck. In the spring of that year the company hired a new office administrator.

To my good fortune the lady they hired was 21 years old, very attractive, and single. I too was single. This story is not about someone being in danger because of a mechanical failure of an airplane; rather, it's about the miracle of romance. It's the story of how the Lord brought two lives together and made it clear to me that I should marry this woman.

Her name was Teresa. As coworkers, we were able to become friends before any thought of developing a romance. She was very kind-hearted and giving. I would call into the office for messages and then ask how her day was going. This went on for several months. Finally, I asked her to go with me to a business reception hosted by a client. She said, "yes," and then she said she also had a reception to attend later that evening. She wanted me to join her. After that, I always enjoyed calling in for messages! In fact, sometimes I called in three times a day! We continued to see each other socially throughout the summer. In August we decided to date each other exclusively.

I had never envisioned myself dating a woman with a child. I did not like the idea of sharing custody, living in a co-parenting situation, or raising children exposed to values different from my own. But Teresa's situation was different—she had been abandoned. She had two children of whom she had full custody. Their biological father had no involvement in their lives.

Teresa's children were ages three and four and they were beautiful. Inexplicably, my heart was changed and I was open to the idea of becoming a ready-made family. Her daughter had special needs; she had moderate cerebral palsy as a result of her premature birth. Yet her smile was so bright and her disposition was so happy that she could melt even the coldest of hearts. She easily melted mine!

I believed that marriage is a lifelong commitment but the idea of being with someone for the rest of my life was very frightening to me. I had never been in love and I didn't know the closeness of having a "one and only." But I thought about her all the time and we had grown to be best friends. On one hand, I was apprehensive. On the other, I wanted to be with her all the time. If I were faced with a major decision today I would make it a matter of prayer and fasting. I didn't have the spiritual insight then that I have now. Nevertheless, the Lord showed me what to do in spite of my young age and my lack of knowledge.

I am a logical person and an accountant by profession; thus, I have always managed my finances carefully. At one point Teresa and I had a "logical" talk about finances to see if we were in agreement. She wasn't as organized as I, so I crafted a simple budget for her. I could see that she had almost no spending money and lived month-to-month, but I still wanted to see if she could live within her means. A few months later she came up significantly short and I didn't understand why. I mentioned it to her but she did not offer me a clear explanation. Of course, I was thinking as an accountant and her lack of explanation bothered me.

One day out of the clear blue, my father asked, "Why don't you have a watch?" I didn't really give it much thought at the time. I told him that I didn't like watches. I'm an active person and watches seem to get in my way. I would break them on the wall or hook them on something. And, I didn't like how flexible bands would flop around on my wrist. So, I solved it all by simply not wearing a watch. What I didn't realize was that my dad was asking me this question for a reason. Without me knowing, Teresa was secretly making payments on a watch she had selected for me for Christmas. That explained why she was short financially. Teresa was trying to keep this sweet gesture a secret. Me? I was clueless and just too insensitive to put those two things together and figure out that she had planned something special just for me.

My desire to be with Teresa grew stronger day by day. But it seemed like this money question went on for several weeks. Each time it came up I would have doubts and I wouldn't get an answer that satisfied me. I began to feel suspicious. Was she lying to me? Was she wasting her money? Could I trust her if our finances were combined? Finally, we had to talk it out. That's when she told me that she had been saving money to buy me a watch for Christmas. I was terribly embarrassed and ashamed of myself for not trusting her. I felt like I was two inches tall. Even worse, my father had already told her that I didn't want to wear a watch. So she had returned the watch to the store two days earlier. I felt so bad that I asked her to go back to the store and purchase it again. *I wanted that watch!* Unfortunately, it had been sold. However, more importantly is that the Lord opened my eyes and showed me that Teresa loved me and that she was His gift to me. The gift that I didn't receive opened my eyes to the bigger gift. After that, I found my peace and I asked Teresa to marry me. I guess I just needed a confirmation and a big shove from the Lord.

In the coming weeks we selected our rings and got engaged on Valentine's Day. (*She* asked *me*, "Can we get engaged on Valentine's Day and will you surprise me?") We set a date for our wedding, rented the beautiful gazebo in Old City Park in Dallas, and asked a minister to do the honors. She bought a beautiful wedding gown and looked stunning. We had a wonderful reception and made plans for a romantic honeymoon to California—San Francisco, Carmel, and Yosemite. I never had another doubt, all because there was no watch!

Because God replaced a small gift with an even greater one, I experienced a tremendous unexpected miracle in my ordinary life.

DISCUSSION QUESTIONS:

1) Does the Lord design a specific man and specific woman for marriage or is it up to us to choose a mate? Can you support your answer with a bible verse or biblical illustration?

_____

_____

_____

_____

_____

2) What is God's purpose (or purposes) for marriage? Why does the Lord bring two people together?

_____

_____

_____

_____

_____

3) Reread the stories of Jacob and Rachel (Genesis 29), Boaz and Ruth (The Book of Ruth), and of David and Abigail (1 Samuel 25). What similarities do you see in the initial stages of their relationships?

_____

_____

_____

_____

_____

For our struggle is not against
flesh and blood,
but against the rulers,
against the powers,
against the world forces of this darkness,
against the spiritual forces
of wickedness in the heavenly places.

Ephesians 6:12 (NASV)

3
FALSELY ACCUSED, YET FREE INDEED!

It was May 5 and just six weeks before our wedding day. Teresa's daughter (my daughter-to-be) was five years old and enrolled in an early childhood development program in the Dallas public schools. Unexpectedly, Teresa received a telephone call from a caseworker with Child Protective Services (CPS) of the State of Texas. She told Teresa that our daughter was in her custody and that she suspected our daughter had been sexually abused. Teresa was terribly shaken and very upset. This couldn't be. What had happened and how? The caseworker wanted to speak with both Teresa and me, and she requested that we bring along her four-year-old son. What they didn't tell her was that I was the suspect!

Together we met with the caseworker and her supervisor and they told us that when our daughter had gone to the bathroom at school, she commented that someone had touched her vaginal area. They called this an "outcry." Then they took custody of our son and talked to him privately, while recording his responses, to determine if he would relate a similar story. They said our daughter had been examined by a state-approved doctor and that he agreed she'd been touched inappropriately. That's when they finally implicated me. I was stunned and shocked. It was as if I was the victim of a witch hunt.

Under the authority of the Texas Family Code, CPS could retain custody of the children until we could have a hearing in a Master's Court, a court created specifically for urgent matters. We were not permitted to see nor talk to the children until the

Master's Court made a ruling. It was a time filled with confusion, anger, and anxiety.

I needed two days to find an attorney. Teresa and I were not married, thus, I was not a party to the hearing and had no standing in the matter. In other words, Teresa's attorney did not represent me. Also, since I was the accused I was not permitted to sit in the court and listen to the proceedings. So first I hired an attorney for Teresa and then, in a preemptive move, I found my own attorney because I fully expected to be charged with a crime I did not commit. My attorney participated in the custody hearing as a "friend of the court." The court appointed an attorney for the children.

Each attorney needed time to prepare, so the hearing was scheduled eleven days after it started. For the next week there was no talk of a wedding. In fact, the whole situation was overwhelmingly difficult to process. None of it was true! It was like a bad nightmare that I just could not awaken from.

Then, with everyone prepared, we proceeded with the hearing in the Master's Court. This was the first time the Lord intervened; the attorneys I hired were excellent and worked as a powerful team. The first bit of testimony, given by the doctor stated that our daughter showed no evidence of physical or sexual abuse. The doctor's testimony made the caseworker's testimony unbelievable. Next we learned that the caseworker had been on the job a mere 10 weeks! We could also see that the claims made by the supervisor were next to impossible to believe. She had a vivid imagination; however, it was just that—her imagination! No evidence existed to back up her claims. It didn't take long for the children's ad litem attorney to side against the CPS.

The Master's Court ordered the children to be returned to their mother immediately. We were very relieved and were ready to hold the children again. We had a moment's hope that our nightmare would quickly come to an end. Unfortunately, that was not what happened.

Despite the Master's Court ruling, the CPS supervisor refused to return the children to us. She demanded that the assistant district attorney go to the district judge to file an appeal. Our attorneys and the ad litem attorney were appalled because this was a direct violation of the law as written plainly in the Texas Family Code. All four attorneys hurried to appear before the district court judge the very next morning for a tense and aggressive hearing. The judge gave firm instructions to the assistant district attorney that the children be returned immediately based on the ruling of the Master Court Judge. Finally, later that afternoon, the CPS caseworker obeyed the court order and the children came home to their mother. Again, we hoped that this would be the end of our nightmare. But once again, it was not. The CPS supervisor demanded that the district attorney pursue a full trial in the district court.

Because of the absurdity of CPS' behavior, our attorneys went on the offensive. This was the second time the Lord's hand moved.

In the previous legislative session, two years earlier, Texas lawmakers created a new law that allowed a civil defense for a frivolous claim brought by a state agency. This was a very narrow remedy that only provided for reimbursement of legal fees incurred in the defense of the case. It did not allow for other monetary damages nor pain and suffering. This was an unusual law because without it, a state cannot be sued because it benefits from sovereign immunity. One of the attorneys was aware of this new law and was willing to take our case on a contingency fee basis; this meant he only got paid if we won. We agreed and thus we began a four-and-a-half year journey through the Texas court system.

More than a year later, and after many hearings and motions, we finally had a trial. The facts were presented as they were in the custody hearing and once again the district court judge ruled in our favor. In addition, he wrote plainly in his opinion that the CPS supervisor and caseworker acted illegally when they ignored the master court ruling, and, for that absurd behavior, brought about a frivolous claim against us. We won a precedent-setting case on the trial court level! We were very excited, but it was still not over.

A first-time or precedent-setting case is always appealed, so next we went to the court of appeals. Legal appeals do not retry the facts of a case. The appeals process examines only the application of law. So, because this was a new law there was no case history to refer to. The justices, a three-judge panel, were free to form their own opinions. They based their opinions on the minutes from the legislative committee that wrote the law and from the wording of the law itself. Unfortunately, the court of appeals ruled against us by a vote of two to one. We were very disappointed and further frustrated because the written opinion included factual inaccuracies made by assumptions of the appeals judge who wrote the opinion.

The final step came with an appeal to the Texas Supreme Court. Most cases are litigated on paper only. However, our case was given the rare opportunity to give oral arguments in front of the full panel of nine Texas Supreme Court Justices. Numerous attorneys practice law their entire career and never have a case heard by the Texas Supreme Court. I also learned that on the higher level things are seldom decided based on the merits of the case or points of law. Instead, decisions are more political.

At that time, the Texas Supreme Court had five Democratic justices and four Republican justices. I'm still not sure why the Democrats supported this new law and the Republicans did not. Nevertheless, we won our appeal to the Texas Supreme Court by a vote of five to four. The justices voted along party lines and the Democrats prevailed over the Republicans. In the next election the Republicans took control of the Texas Supreme Court. If our case had been heard five months later, we would have lost because of partisan voting. Once again, the Lord's timing was perfect.

I never ever expected to be falsely accused of something as absurd as child abuse nor be party to a lawsuit that went all the way to the Texas Supreme Court. Nevertheless, I was. Two Dallas newspaper articles were printed about the case and I was on the television news three times and on the radio twice. Our attorneys were featured on the cover of a statewide legal magazine, as the case had significant legal ramifications in the legal community.

More than 20 years later I gave testimony to a class at a large church. After the class, I was introduced to a man who worked as an advocate for fathers' rights in custody cases involving allegations of this kind. So I asked if he'd heard of our case. He responded without hesitation, "Yes, I know that case. We use it all the time!"

I am as concerned as anyone when I hear of child abuse. It is an emotionally charged topic that is filled with many complexities. I stand against child abuse but I also stand in support of responsible investigation of these cases, not witch hunts. CPS caseworkers are trained as social workers, not as police officers or lawyers. These boundaries must be respected.

I believe that this experience was Satan's attempt to destroy my family before Teresa and I stood at the marriage altar. He was certainly not pleased that we were becoming a family and that the kids would be raised in a Christian home and with Biblical values. What Satan intended for evil, God intended for good on a much larger scale.

Yes, God showed up with yet another unexpected miracle in my ordinary life.

DISCUSSION QUESTIONS:

1) What factors would lead you to turn the other cheek to a conflict and what factors would lead you to stand your ground and fight for what you know is right?

_____

_____

_____

_____

_____

2) Do all battles occur because of spiritual conflict or do some conflicts occur because of our own actions? Consider Exodus 20:5 and Psalm 38:3 in your answer.

_____

_____

_____

_____

_____

3) What are biblically appropriate ways to respond to conflict and what are unbiblical and inappropriate ways? Consider Matthew 5:23-26, John 8:2-11, and Matthew 18:15-35.

_____

_____

_____

_____

_____

When you pass through the waters,
I will be with you;
And through the rivers, they will not
overflow you.
When you walk through the fire,
you will not be
scorched, nor will the flame burn you.

Isaiah 43:2 (NASV)

4
ICY TEXAS ROADS IN JUNE!

S aturday, June 10, 1989. I remember the date well because it was the day before my first wedding anniversary. My wife, Teresa, and I had plans for a romantic dinner that evening. My parents agreed to watch the kids beginning at lunchtime so that Teresa and I could have time to ourselves. It was a day to be thankful. However, the attorneys asked us to meet with them because a hearing was scheduled the next week regarding the frivolous lawsuit. So it was necessary to drive to downtown Dallas for a morning meeting before heading to my parents' house in East Dallas. I had an extra errand to run before the lawyer meeting, so Teresa and I decided it would be easier to drive two cars and meet up at the attorney's office. Teresa had the kids with her, along with their overnight things. It was a busy day but we were excited about our plans.

The central business district of Dallas is encircled by a network of highways. One section is at ground level, another section is elevated, and yet another section is uncovered but below grade. Everyone refers to the section that's below grade as "The Canyon." When you're driving through the area there are high concrete walls on both sides and it feels as if you're in a hole. It's not a place to relax; it's noisy and busy. In fact, all of the highways in that area are busy no matter the time of day.

Texas is famous for its rapid changes in weather. In the spring and summer months, thunderstorms can appear and disappear within a few hours. The morning is not the usual time for a shower; nevertheless, on that day a thunderstorm had built over the downtown area and brought with it a nice refreshing shower. It cooled the downtown area and rained in the canyon.

I was good with directions because I had lived in Dallas my entire life and had the roads memorized. So when I left the attorney's office I drove to the nearest highway entrance. It took me down and through the canyon as I'd driven many times before. I drove a small Toyota sports truck. As I turned and drove down the ramp I noticed that the freeway was unusually quiet at that particular moment; there were no cars in front of me for more than 100 yards. What I didn't expect was how the rain had mixed with all the dirt and oil on the road. It was screaming danger!

Since no cars were ahead of me the water on the road stood undisturbed. It was smooth as water on a pond with no breeze. To a light-weight truck, this was quite treacherous because it was actually as slick as ice even if it was June. I estimated that I was driving approximately 60 mph when my tires began to hydroplane on the thin layer of water. Those moments are forever imprinted in my mind in slow motion. I was in the center lane and my truck drifted left. I turned the steering wheel slightly to the right and in the direction that I was moving but my response made no difference, I had no traction. I was out of control and totally caught by surprise.

In an instant my truck was sliding off the road to the left. My rear tires were hydroplaning and had no traction. They had moved to the right so that I was sliding down the road sideways at a 50-degree angle or so, while drifting toward the center median. Only one section of the canyon did not have a center guardrail to separate lanes; unfortunately, I was at that section at that exact moment, so my truck continued sailing across the median and into the oncoming traffic.

In less than a few seconds, I collided with two cars traveling in the opposite direction. It was a high-impact crash with all of us driving in the 50 mph range. My truck was still at an angle when it collided with the oncoming cars so they made impact with the passenger side of my truck. One car made a glancing blow to the front section; one made impact with the passenger door. My truck was wrecked beyond recognition.

It looked as if I should have been killed in the wreckage.

The impact left me stunned and I momentarily blacked out. I can remember the loud bang of the metal cars crashing. When I opened my eyes I saw that I was covered in thousands of giblets of broken windshield glass. All the cars on the freeway came to a complete stop. Miraculously, I unfastened my seatbelt, got out of the truck and walked to the grassy embankment beside the road and sat down until my head cleared.

As I sat on the grass my body was temporarily numb. I sat physically frozen; yet, a million thoughts flooded my mind. In one moment the fear of the events of the impact was almost too overwhelming; then, I had a feeling of embarrassment because of the traffic jam I'd caused. I felt relief, too, that it was over, and then amazement that I was alive! The event was quite surreal. I wanted to talk to my wife and I wanted to hug the children. I was breathless, numb, and even confused about what I should do next.

Traffic was tangled for hours in both directions.

I sat on the embankment as emergency vehicles arrived. Someone I didn't know offered me a cell phone so I could call my father. He answered promptly, knew exactly where I was in the canyon, and soon appeared driving on the shoulder of the highway to the accident scene. I felt an incredible sense of relief when I saw my dad because I was simply overwhelmed by the situation. I almost broke into tears. Finally, someone I trusted without question! Finally, someone who would help me!

The paramedics talked to me and the others. They checked me over to see if I was okay. I thought I was fine but when my father arrived, he gave me a hug which caused a piercing pain in my chest. So the paramedics looked me over again and insisted, along with my dad, that I get in the ambulance to go to the hospital for examination. I don't remember much after that because they sedated me for the transport to the hospital.

At the hospital the doctors examined me and ordered me to take a test that checked my heart for injury. It checked out to be okay, but when they x-rayed me they found that I had five broken ribs and a collapsed right lung. Although I was wearing my safety belt, it now appeared that I'd hit the steering wheel in the collision. I remained in the hospital for five days. Obviously we had to postpone our wedding anniversary dinner until later.

I have no doubt that the Lord preserved my life that day. All the events I endured usually lead to a tragic result. Yes, it was another unexpected miracle in my ordinary life and for that I am so very grateful. Yet, as I reflect on that day there was much more to it than God just sparing my life.

When we left the morning meeting with the attorney, I'd asked the children if they wanted to ride with me or with their mother to their grandparents' house. They were six and five at the time and typically one would ride with me and the other with their mom. But on that day, they both said without hesitation, "We want to ride with Mom."

Small trucks such as the one I drove are not very wide. You can reach across and touch the passenger door without stretching too far. After the collision the passenger door was literally in the middle of the truck and the passenger seat was completely destroyed. There is no doubt that a person riding with me would have been killed instantly. I shiver all over when I think that one of my children could have been riding with me. I hadn't experienced one miracle that day; I experienced two! I believe the Holy Spirit of God intervened and whispered a thought in their minds when I asked them who they wanted to ride with. I thank the Lord for saving my life that day, but even more, I thank Him for protecting my children and preserving their little lives.

Isaiah 43:2 tells us that Isaiah passed through the waters and the fire and was *not* injured. On that Saturday in June, I experienced two incredible unexpected miracles in my ordinary life.

DISCUSSION QUESTIONS:

1) Think back over your life. In hindsight, what are times when the Lord has protected you or directed you and you didn't realize it at the time?

_____

_____

_____

_____

_____

2) Colossians 1:17 says, *"He is before all things, and in Him all things hold together."* In addition to our protection, in what other ways does the Lord hold all things together? (Consider this from many perspectives such as medical, scientific, and environmental.)

_____

_____

_____

_____

_____

3) How frequently should we thank the Lord for His protection? What is the Lord's response to our gratitude? Have you thanked Him recently?

_____

_____

_____

_____

God's way is perfect.
All the LORD's promises prove true.
He is a shield for all who look to Him
for protection.

Psalm 18:30 (NLT)

5
A SPECIALIZED SURGERY LED BY THE HAND OF GOD

After we married, I adopted Teresa's two children. Although I was not present at her birth, our daughter was born 10 weeks premature. She was a tiny 5 pounds and 4 ounces, suffered a stroke during birth, and had a collapsed lung. Her little body was just not ready to be born. As a result she suffered oxygen deprivation to the brain, which resulted in injury. This is called cerebral palsy (CP).

CP can manifest itself in different ways depending on the location of the injury and the brain function affected. Our daughter is afflicted in her limbs. She cannot walk without the assistance of a walker or crutches. Her hands were also affected so she cannot perform tasks that require fine motor skills. We had her tested to determine her skill level and learned that she is unable to drive; she can't control her hands and arms well enough to operate a vehicle.

CP is not a condition that grows worse nor is it contagious. The damage that occurs at birth is final. Oftentimes, persons affected by CP experience an increase in their quality of life as they age because they gradually learn how to overcome their limitations. Our society is quite accepting of persons with such limitations by providing easy access to buildings and parking, offering public transportation with special accommodations, and employing advanced technologies to make life in general easier.

When our daughter was seven years old we took her to a regularly scheduled checkup at the Scottish Rite Hospital for Children in Dallas. The Scottish Rite Hospitals provide the best care possible for kids with special needs, from any place in the world. And what's even more amazing is that these facilities provide this care at no cost to the patient's family. Hospital staff assisted us in several ways, such as routinely resizing our daughter's leg braces and providing other equipment such as walkers and crutches.

They even helped us with future problems that could deter her as she grew. And, when our daughter was 12 a bone was grafted from her thigh and fused to the inside of each foot. The purpose of this procedure was to retain her feet so that they would not roll under as she grew into adulthood.

At this particular appointment the orthopedic doctor, Dr. Charles Johnston, made a recommendation that we take our daughter to be evaluated for a specialized surgery.

The surgery, "rhizotomy," is performed by neurological doctors who open the spinal cord and stimulate the nerves while at the same time monitoring the response of those nerves. Then the surgeons selectively sever any nerves deemed to be "problematic."

CP causes involuntary muscle contraction in many patients. For some, this involuntary contraction (or muscle spasms) can be very painful and even severe enough to pull bones out of socket. By cutting the nerves, the inappropriate brain signal is broken and spasticity is reduced. The goal of the surgery is for patients to be more comfortable and have fewer spasms.

Teresa and I took our daughter to be evaluated. The doctors recommended the procedure, but Teresa and I labored over the decision. Our daughter was too young to understand the risks so we didn't ask for her opinion; however, we knew if something went wrong it could mean that she would spend the rest of her life confined to a wheelchair. We met with the neurosurgeons, Dr. Eric Sklar and Dr. Derek Bruce of Medical City Hospital in Dallas and learned that they were well-respected worldwide. (Years later these doctors would be acclaimed for participating with the team that separated two conjoined Egyptian boys.) After much prayer and discussion we decided to proceed.

The surgery went as planned and there were no complications. However, the moment I saw my daughter after surgery my first thought was, "They didn't do enough." I could see as she rested in the bed that spasticity still remained in her hands, arms, and legs. At that moment I was a bit disappointed but I kept my thoughts to myself.

Surgery was followed by a recovery period and then a year of weekly physical therapy sessions. This great amount of therapy time was required to properly evaluate the effectiveness of the surgery.

Rhizotomy was a relatively new procedure at the time. We were certainly not among the first to be recommended for the surgery, but it was a time when the doctors were learning more and more with each case, refining the procedure, and being more selective with the patients they recommended to have the surgery. Dr. Johnston later explained to us that spasticity is actually helpful to some CP patients. Without it many simply fall to the ground because they do not have enough normal muscle control to stand; so, over-aggressive rhizotomy results could mean they are bedridden for life. A few years later I met a man whose daughter had undergone the surgery and he was strongly opposed to it, so it's not for every CP patient. First, would it reduce unwanted spasticity? Secondly, which nerves should or should not be severed before it caused more problems than it solved? The procedure was technically sound and beneficial however; in some cases, it could be harmful if too many nerves were severed.

After the recovery and the extended physical therapy we returned to Scottish Rite Hospital for another checkup. Dr. Johnston examined our daughter. He knew her well because he was the only surgeon who attended to her during our treatment years. He asked her to stand and walk and he checked her range of motion. Then he stepped back and said, "Of all the rhizotomy patients we've had, I think you are the best." He was very pleased with her abilities and the surgery results. He had a big smile and an uncharacteristically festive tone in his voice. She had enough muscle control to walk upright with a walker or with crutches and she had reduced spasticity. Doctors Sklar and Bruce had made the correct decisions.

The scriptures say, *"God's way is perfect. All the Lord's promises prove true. He is a shield for all who look to Him for protection."* (Psalm 18:30, NLT) What I thought to be "not enough" was actually the perfect amount. The Lord's hand was on the doctors that day and the result was a lifelong blessing to our daughter.

As I look back on that time, I know I witnessed another unexpected miracle in my ordinary life.

DISCUSSION QUESTIONS:

1) Consider the complexities of our bodies (the spinal cord, the brain stem, the right/left brain synapse, the optic nerve, etc.). What does this complexity communicate about our Heavenly Father?

_____

_____

_____

_____

2) Considering that the Lord is perfect, what spiritual purpose is accomplished by or through someone who has a physical affliction? Who is ultimately affected by the affliction? What unique spiritual gifts may an afflicted person have (see 1 Corinthians 12:4-11)? What unique fruits of the Spirit, gifts, or talents may result from the presence of an affliction within a family?

_____

_____

_____

_____

3) The Lord is perfect in all His ways (Psalm 18:30). What is an appropriate response when we recognize that the Lord's provisions for us are perfect?

_____

_____

_____

_____

Yet you do not know what your life will be like tomorrow. You are just a vapor that appears for a little while and then vanishes away.

James 4:14 (NASV)

6
A CORD REPAIRED

I've been going to the lake since I was two years old. My parents were best friends with the Crawford family and they liked to go to the lake too. During the summer we went on Sunday afternoons after church. My dad always found the perfect spot in the park and my mom spread quilts out on the ground next to the water's edge. There we'd all have a scrumptious picnic. Both of our families owned boats so we'd invite many friends and water ski until dusk. Our dads always had a friendly skiing competition to determine the number one skier! That contest has lasted for more than four decades and there's no end in sight.

I remember playing by the water when I was as young as five. My favorite memory is of a blue molded plastic toy boat, about 18 inches long. It was stamped PT-109 and was made to resemble the boat that President John F. Kennedy commanded in World War II. It was a good boat for me because of its size; as a little boy I had to use two hands to carry it. I thought it was big and I was proud of it. One day the wind blew it out into the deep water and I was so afraid that I would lose it. My dad and his ski boat, however, came to my rescue and retrieved my prized possession!

Over the years times changed and the lake areas became more developed and populated. Eventually, the Crawford family bought a lake house. Now we had a specific place to go to and we could spend the night at the lake. Spending the night was an occasional pleasure that created special memories. Lakes are made for boys because there is always a fish to be caught, a turtle to be found, or a snake to scare the girls. July Fourth is always a time to set off fireworks and stay up late. And, baked beans and hamburger meat cooking on the grill were ever-present aromas at mealtime.

When I was in high school the Crawford family moved away so my parents decided to purchase lake property for our family. A few years later, after I graduated college and had a job, my parents and I built a small house on the property. It was nice to go there to escape the city and enjoy the peace and quiet of the lake. It was a welcomed change to sleep with the windows open and listen to the frogs and other night sounds. I loved the smell of the lake floating in our windows each morning. That aroma was just as refreshing as the smell of cinnamon rolls and biscuits coming from the kitchen. We often drove to our property on Fridays and returned to our city home on Sundays. We would be sunburned and tired, but refreshed and eager for the new week.

In the late 90s my dad still owned his boat. However, jet skis had become a more popular way to get around on the lake. I just had to have one. Teresa and I decided to buy a new SeaDoo built for two. It was powerful enough to pull a skier or an inner tube and small enough to drive in and out of our waterfront property. It was easy to maintain and everyone enjoyed it immensely. The kids were even permitted to drive as long as an adult rode with them.

One weekend we arrived after dark on Friday night. Since it was late we unloaded our things but left the SeaDoo parked on the trailer by the road. All the personal water craft made in the 90s and early 2000s were two-stroke engines. This meant they were different from cars because they didn't have an alternator to keep the battery charged. At the end of the day it was possible that the battery would go dead from mere usage. So I kept a battery charger at the lake house and recharged the battery each night before going to bed. To hook up a battery charger I needed an extension cord. We had several in our shed, and on this trip it was dark, so I grabbed the easiest one to find, fumbled with a flashlight, attached the charger to the battery and left it for the night.

It was an unalienable right to sleep late at the lake house so I lingered in bed the next morning, had a leisurely breakfast, and then went to unhook the charger and prepare the SeaDoo to be put in the water. I didn›t pay any particular attention to the extension cord I had used; however, it was one that had been repaired. My dad had spliced a new plug into the cord. It was well taped and we had used it many times before without any problem. If we had known it was defective, the cord would have been put in the garbage without a second thought. Nevertheless, when I disconnected the cord from the battery charger I quickly found that I had a problem. The opposite end of the extension cord remained plugged into the outside wall socket so it was still hot with an electrical current. When I grabbed the cord I unknowingly grabbed the spliced section with my left hand. What I didn't know was that a wire in the extension cord had poked through the black electrical tape. When my hand made contact with the wire, the electrical current jumped from the wire to my left hand, went down my arm, and through my leg to the ground. Instantly I fell to the ground, my hand muscles constricted tightly in the current and, thus, caused me to grab the cord even tighter. My left leg and arm muscles also constricted. Electrical current running through a human body causes muscles to constrict out of control—thus, the power of the current was stronger than I was! My entire left side was buzzing with intensity. In the blink of an eye I was being electrocuted!

I don't know how much time passed, perhaps as much as two minutes, but I was helpless! All I could do was to yell and hope that Teresa heard me in the house and would come help me. The kids said I yelled three times and even the neighbors said they heard me. As I lay on the ground on my left side, I felt my right leg free of the current and contractions. I don't remember consciously thinking about it because it all happened so fast, but instinctively I kicked my right leg. After a couple of kicks I was able to hook the extension cord with my right foot and kick hard enough for the cord to pull loose from the wall socket. At the same moment it fell from the socket, Teresa was there. She could see what was happening to me and was rushing to unplug the cord.

I'm not an electrician nor a doctor so I have no idea how long I could have withstood that electrical current before my heart gave out. I was healthy and strong and in my early 40s, but I don't think I could have taken much more than what I did. That brief minute or two left me shaken and exhausted. Teresa helped me back into the house and I rested until the afternoon. I felt the effects of the electricity all day. And, I was left with a small burn hole on my hand, which is still a scar to this day. It wasn't until the next day that my energy returned and I felt normal again.

We take our tomorrows for granted. But life is fragile and can vanish in the blink of an eye. Fortunately, on that day at the lake the Lord protected me. I experienced yet another unexpected miracle in my ordinary life.

DISCUSSION QUESTIONS:

1) What brief moments in your life have had lasting impact?

_____

_____

_____

_____

_____

2) Ultimately, how extensive is your power over circumstances such as disease or injury? How does this compare to God's power?

_____

_____

_____

_____

_____

3) Read Psalm 90:12 and ask yourself, "If my life were to end today how would I feel about the way I've spent my days?"

_____

_____

_____

_____

_____

*Every good thing given and every
perfect gift is from above,
coming down from the Father of lights,
with whom there is no variation or
shifting shadow.*

James 1:17 (NASV)

7
WE'RE TWINS!

Six months before we were married, Teresa, my bride-to-be, suffered from endometriosis and an ovarian cyst. The doctors recommended surgery and said Teresa would be unable to conceive more children; however, she'd have a better quality of life. In all sincerity and kindness toward me, Teresa said that she'd understand if I did not want to follow through with our wedding plans because of her inability to bear children.

Her health issues were not a concern to me as my mother had dealt with similar problems and I was familiar with the scenario. Teresa already had two beautiful children and the four of us were behaving as a family unit even before our wedding. For me, it was just another bump in the road. And, I had health concerns of my own—recurring sinus infections that were often debilitating. I didn't want to father a child if the possibility existed for him or her to inherit my physical struggles. So Teresa decided to have the surgery and we considered our family complete. We were content with our decision.

In our eighth year of marriage Teresa's cousin became pregnant. This cousin was single and already the parent of a toddler of whom she did not have full custody.

She also did not believe that abortion was an option for her fetus. Family members encouraged her to have the baby and then allow Teresa and me to adopt it. Unfortunately, she didn't like their suggestions and instead contacted an adoption agency in her city where she was introduced to a nice couple.

During the next six months she proceeded with the adoption process and drafted all the legal documents. Then came the day for her to sign the papers to terminate her parental rights. At that point she and her mother, Teresa's aunt, realized that this young mother-to-be would no longer have contact with the child. This termination of rights bothered her greatly. The grandmother had strong objections as well. So the young mother had a change of heart and was determined to raise the child herself with the support of the child's grandmother.

When we first learned of this pregnancy in our extended family, Teresa and I discussed adopting the child. We liked the idea and thought that having a newborn baby would be a blessing, but we heard that Teresa's cousin had objections, so we dismissed the baby idea. We knew these types of decisions, especially with young mothers, were tumultuous. And, we did not care to live on an emotional roller coaster ride, so we put the subject out of our minds and considered it a closed matter.

The baby was born November 27—a healthy and precious boy. However, out of concern and caution, the doctors wanted the baby to receive more oxygen and be monitored for sleep apnea during his first month of life. This extra care was somewhat demanding and the birth mother found it to be unmanageable. After a few days of attending to beeping equipment, checking monitors, and responding to frequent alarms, she had a change of heart and decided it was best that she not continue to mother the child.

Once again, family members encouraged her to give the child to Teresa and me so that he could remain in the family. The grandmother wanted to share his life and she was adamant that the baby remain in the family. So that's when Teresa received the call from her cousin. I was never privy to all that was discussed, but, it was one of those breathless moments. The second they hung up, Teresa called me at work and said in her soft voice, "Klay, she's asked me if we want the baby." "Was she serious?" I asked. Teresa answered in an unmistakable tone, "Yes, she was." I think there is an unspoken understanding between women about the seriousness of motherhood.

Teresa and her cousin had made a connection. So I told her, "Yes, I want that baby!" Teresa wanted him too so I told her to pack the car and prepare to go get him.

We were excited beyond description! Teresa loaded the car and along with our older daughter made the five-hour drive to the cousin's home. The baby needed more medical attention so Teresa lingered a few days before she could return to our home. Finally, with a new car seat secured, infant diapers, tiny clothing, and bottles of formula she made the trip home. I had never seen Teresa more radiant than the day she walked through the door with our new baby in her arms. She was absolutely beautiful. God was good.

We experienced an unexpected miracle in our ordinary life. We named our miracle Blake!

If I were given the opportunity to relive certain days of my life, I would choose the time when Blake was born until the time he began first grade. Those years went by much too fast. Every day was filled with precious moments: the day he first lifted his head, the day he rolled over for the first time, the day he first stood, and the day he began to walk. And, of course, Christmas is always more festive when children are in the house!

One of my favorite memories was when we had a small wading pool. We put it in the backyard at the bottom of the plastic yellow slide, which was part of Blake's playground set. He was about three years old and he wore an orange and blue Speedo swimsuit with "Snoopy" written across his little bottom. He had so much fun that day that he didn't want to stop! For me it was more than fun; I experienced the joy of fatherhood. Our older kids loved little Blake too.

Blake and I are similar in many ways. Our hair color is the same and we both have a slender build. He enjoyed playing soccer as I did. And, even our personalities are similar; he always thinks he's the boss and I must remind him frequently that I am the dad and that he is the son. He's confident, outgoing, and very agile in athletics. If you were to see us side-by-side, you'd think we were biological father and son.

My sweet Teresa fell terminally ill when Blake was six. The Lord took her home to be with Him when Blake was eight years old. This was the darkest season of my life. As I reflect on the days that followed Teresa's passing, I remember the deep depression that accompanied my grief. Most mornings I did not want to get out of bed. I wanted to just lie there until I died. And I would have stayed in my bed except for the fact that I had one unavoidable responsibility—an energetic and playful eight-year-old boy who would walk into my room all dressed in his little boy clothes, backpack perched on his back, and all ready for school! He was in the second grade and loved it. In the months and years to follow, Blake suffered many moments when he missed his mother and he certainly grieved. However, he was also a healthy, vibrant little boy and he had a huge appetite for life.

When I look back on that difficult season in my life, I see that Blake's presence in my life not only gave me a reason to get out of bed, but gave me reason to carry on with my life. What I didn't understand until later is that the Lord had given me this precious gift a long time before I knew I'd need it! God's timing was perfect and Blake's presence in my life was God's provision for me at that season in my life.

How many people do you know who have been blessed with a child when they were unable to have one of their own? For me, the miracle of a child in my life had a much deeper purpose that was not truly evident until a future time. The scripture says, "Every perfect gift is from above, coming down from the Father of lights" (James 1:17).

There's no doubt that I received a perfect gift from God, which was an awesome unexpected miracle in my ordinary life.

DISCUSSION QUESTIONS:

1) What is the best gift you've received for your birthday, graduation, or Christmas? What are the best gifts this world can offer?

_____

_____

_____

_____

_____

2) Read James 1:12-17. How are "Gifts from above" unique in the purposes they serve? How are they different from the gifts you've listed in the first question? What would your Heavenly Father consider a perfect gift for you?

_____

_____

_____

_____

_____

3) Read Ester 4:14. Has the Lord given you a gift before you needed it? In what ways has the Lord's work in your life been present before you knew it?

_____

_____

_____

_____

_____

*For I know the plans that
I have for you,"
declares the LORD, "plans
for welfare and not
for calamity to give you a
future and a hope.*

Jeremiah 29:11 (NASV)

8
ACHIEVING THE AMERICAN DREAM!

When I was in my late 30s, I began to feel restless in my career and dissatisfied with my income. It was time to go in a new direction. It was my turn to pursue the American Dream. I wanted to own a business!

I approached this desire with my typical business logic. My first step was to evaluate various business opportunities. I wanted something that would be as much of an investment as it was a business; I desired to be more of an owner and manager than employee. So I began the tedious task of researching opportunities that ranged from restaurants to laundromats. The business that appealed to me the most was a quick oil change, auto inspection, and auto repair business. It was a business that I knew I could learn quickly and it did not require a professional license to own.

Many successful quick oil change businesses were already in operation and it was a proven industry. To my good fortune I saw a sign for a new oil change business, which was being constructed three miles from my home. It was not a franchised business, but it had a good name that was shared with other reputable businesses of the same kind. A development company was selling the business, as well as offering training and support.

I wanted to know more so I called the phone number on the sign and then met the president of the development company. He was an older, Southern gentleman who seemed genuine and honest. He was "old school" and believed that a man's word and handshake were as good as a contract.

In our first meeting at his office, we discussed the industry in general; he answered my questions, and then told me of his own company's success story. I felt as if we became instant friends because we both had an entrepreneurial spirit. In a second phone call we discussed more specific information about the location of the new business. He told me that the business near my house was indeed available for purchase. The plan then was that he would leave a packet of financial and legal information about the business at his office. I agreed to pick up the packet from the front desk on my way home Wednesday night. I would then review the information over the weekend and get back to him the following Monday, after having several days to read the information and consider all that business-ownership would encompass.

Wednesday turned into a hectic business day. I was needed at a client's office and from there I knew it would be a long drive to the development company. And, I stayed late that day at the office and didn't get home until after 7:30 p.m. Since all this was unexpected I was unable to stop by during business hours to retrieve the packet as I'd promised. I didn't think it was a big deal since we had agreed that I would read the literature over the weekend, so, I just stopped by the next day, Thursday, instead.

As it turned out, what I thought was not a big deal was indeed significant to the company president. The next morning he looked to see if I had come by as we discussed. I did not know it at the time, but he was testing me. When he saw the literature packet still laying on the front desk, he assumed I was not serious about the business opportunity. When I finally picked up the packet later that day, he was out of the office and I was unable to speak with him.

I did as I'd promised and reviewed the literature that weekend and called him Monday as I'd planned all along. I said I'd read the details and that I'd like to pursue the purchase of that particular quick oil change business. He quickly stopped me and said he had met with another man the Friday before. He said the other man had also wanted this particular location. He went on to say that because I'd not picked up the literature Wednesday as was my original intent, he assumed I'd changed my mind and so he decided to talk to the other man. As it turned out, they signed a contract and exchanged money all in one day, the Friday they met! This was rather unusual and, I was disappointed to lose my dream, but I had no choice but to accept it and move on.

The company president apologized that it did not work out, but knowing that I was truly serious, offered to show me two other available locations up for sale; unfortunately, they were not as conveniently located to my home. Within the next few weeks I checked them out and determined that they too were good business opportunities. They all had a history and were actually less risky than starting a new business. So I chose one of these locations and within six weeks was the proud owner of my own quick oil change business. This type of purchase was a turnkey business opportunity and included the purchase of the land, building, equipment, and inventory. And, by buying an existing business, I had trained personnel already working. The down payment was $125,000, which was a large investment to me.

I owned that business for five years. However, I frequently thought of the first location because I drove by it often. I often wondered if I'd made the right decision. I wondered if the new location was more financially successful than the existing business I'd purchased. Then one day I had a conversation with a staff member at the development company. I casually mentioned the location near my home and asked how it was doing. I don't believe that person realized my true reason for asking; he probably just thought I was being friendly. I learned from him, however, that the owner of that new business had failed and lost his money.

Part of the risk of owning a new business of that kind is determining if the neighborhood surrounding the store can indeed support the business. And, it takes time to build a clientele. When a location fails the development company usually takes over the operation. Under this arrangement it's not visible to the public when a business fails because the doors never close and business never stops; development company employees are sent in to operate the business until a new owner can be found.

As for that original location that I wanted, the first owner lost his investment. Then a second owner purchased the business and after three years it failed again. I did not keep track of the performance of the business after the second failing, but at a minimum it has had three owners and two of them lost $125,000 or more. By comparison, the business I purchased had plenty of challenges; however, I did not lose my investment.

As I reflect on the circumstances surrounding the business decision I made and how my direction changed in an instant because I was unable to pick up the literature as initially planned, I realized that I could have easily been the first person to buy the new business and I could have eventually lost my investment. For that I am grateful.

The Lord had protected me in business by sending me in a new direction. I didn't even know it at the time. The events surrounding my business ownership were neither glamorous nor dangerous, but the way the Lord orchestrated the circumstances was clearly an unexpected miracle in my ordinary life.

DISCUSSION QUESTIONS:

1) Think about Joseph (the son of Jacob) and how his life changed in one day. Also consider Moses as a baby, drifting in the reeds, and how his life changed in an instant. What other Bible characters' lives changed quickly? In what ways has the Lord redirected you in an instant? How do we know when the Lord is orchestrating a change in our life or when we should stay the course?

_____

_____

_____

_____

2) People say, "God's timing is not our timing." What Bible verses or Bible stories do you know that support the idea of "God's timing"?

_____

_____

_____

_____

3) Read Psalm 147:1-5 and consider why the Lord is concerned with the details of your life. What other verses communicate the Lord's personal concern for your life?

_____

_____

_____

_____

～∾

No weapon that is formed
against you will prosper.

Isaiah 54:17 (NASV)

～∾

9
UNEXPECTED PROVISIONS

It is true. Being the owner of your own business is the American Dream. For some people this means success that leads to financial independence and freedom; however, for others the result is not so profitable. Sometimes businesses fail. My business venture did not fail; however, being a business owner meant that I worked many long hours for minimal pay and faced challenges I'd not known.

The first thing I learned was that typical employees at an oil change business are unreliable. It's not a high paying job. One third of the employees in the industry have criminal records and have served time in a penitentiary. Another third have served jail time for crimes such as public intoxication, unpaid traffic tickets, or domestic issues. The final third are reliable and honest; however, they can be easily influenced by those in the first two groups.

On a Tuesday following Memorial Day, about six weeks after I bought the store, only one of my seven employees showed up for work. That day I personally changed the oil in customer cars with the help of my one employee, my father, and my fourteen-year-old son. During the next few months I experienced for the first time how to terminate employees. I fired them for theft, poor attendance, and refusal to perform their duties. Having reliable and trained employees was absolutely necessary to keep my business running smoothly.

I also learned that dealing with certain types of customers could be quite challenging. Some customers seemed to purposely target our business. One woman came in for an oil change for her car. I seriously doubt that her vehicle had ever been serviced and it had been driven more than 70,000 miles! The motor was filthy on the outside and a gummy mess on the inside. A few days later she returned with her husband claiming that the motor was damaged because of the oil change we'd performed. I listened to their concern and explained to the husband that the oil had indeed been changed properly. I then pointed out to him all the evidence of neglect and told him that he needed to prove with receipts and service history that indeed the car had been serviced regularly. If the history could be determined, I explained, then we could talk about the mechanical problems and determine a settlement regarding the alleged damage he claimed we caused.

When he saw that I was not to be easily taken and that he must provide proof, he changed his tone. He came to understand that the problem with his motor was not a result of a mere oil change, but of his own negligence in maintaining the vehicle over its lifetime.

On another occasion a car owner left our building after an oil change, ran an errand, and then went home. When the owner drove the car into his driveway, it began to burn and the fire department was called to the rescue. The car was a total loss and my workers were blamed for the fire. The next day I called the insurance company and a fire investigator was sent out. He was highly trained and very thorough, and determined that the fire began in the engine compartment in front of the passenger seat. Most likely, he reported, the fire was caused by leaves that had fallen into the heater core from the vent below the passenger-side wiper blade. The fire had nothing to do with the oil change. Nevertheless, the insurance company paid the claim of $3500 to the vehicle owner, because, even though there was no mistake on our part, defending the claim in court would have cost much more than $3500 in legal fees. As it is in the insurance world, events such as this result in increased insurance premiums and I suffered the brunt of this fiasco. My insurance premiums immediately increased because of something that had nothing to do with our work.

The quick oil and lube business is a management-intensive, fast-paced business. Everyone who walked into the door wanted something. Vendors had demands and there was little I could do if they wanted to increase wholesale prices. A large competing corporation built a new store in my area, which led to a decrease in my daily car count. Even that city government gave little support to small businesses such as mine. Frequent visits from various inspectors led me to believe that my business was being "overregulated." After all, I was indeed spending a lot of time adhering to compliance rules and regulations.

At the three-year mark as a business owner, I had only earned a small profit. I was nearing a critical point where my working capital was depleted and cash flow problems were lurking around the corner. I had a large property tax bill coming due and I didn't have the money to pay it. The summer heat in Texas was draining and I was physically tired. I was at my wits end and did not know what to do to make the store more profitable. Sales numbers showed little improvement after I changed signage and tried the direct mail approach. I even met with a bankruptcy attorney to see if he could provide options. And, I remember praying Isaiah 54:17, *"No weapon that is formed against you will prosper."* This verse is God's promise that I was already a *victor* and not a *victim* in the many challenges I faced. That difficult season served to strengthen my faith and proved to me that many life circumstances are only temporary and change for the better as time passes.

One day a young, smart-looking man came into the store looking for a job. He related that he'd just moved in with his mother and lived a few blocks from the store. "I'm close enough to walk to work," he said proudly. He was educated, articulate, and seemed to be over-qualified for the role of oil changer. I didn't need an additional employee at that moment, and, honestly, I felt suspicious. However, he offered to work for free for one week and then I'd decide if I wanted to hire him permanently. Just his humble offer showed me that he had the personality of a great salesman. Perhaps he could help us, I thought, so I decided to give him a try.

As it turned out, he had several years of experience at an identical oil change business in another city. He made me see what I'd been missing and he helped increase the amount of sales per car. Because of this one employee's contributions, the average revenue per car increased nearly ten dollars. So, ten dollars multiplied by thirty-five cars per day added up quickly and contributed greatly to my bottom line. This employee also successfully trained other employees for after he was no longer on my staff, the average revenue per car remained at a high level.

The young man worked with me for about five months. After I got to know him I learned that he had a cocaine addiction which had been very destructive in his life. He had moved in with his mother because he had nowhere else to go; he had lost his driver license and needed a job within walking distance.

I felt compassion for him and wanted to help. Unfortunately, cocaine is a problem that some people never overcome. He needed help that was beyond my ability to provide. His employment ended when he drove off in a customer's car because he was looking to satisfy his craving. This illegal and stupid action put me in a very difficult situation, retrieving the car and explaining to the customer what had happened to his vehicle.

Without regard to this young man's personal problems, he was still a great help in improving the performance of my business. After a short period of increased sales, my cash flow was so improved that I was able to pay my property taxes on time. And, I was able to meet my cash needs until I sold the store.

I've oftentimes wondered about that young man. Just what were the chances that a person would happen to walk in off the street and provide me the exact help that I needed at the exact time I needed it? I believe the Lord provided for my needs from this very unlikely source. Yes, even this provision from God was yet another unexpected miracle in my rather ordinary life.

DISCUSSION QUESTIONS:

1) Read the story of Joseph in Genesis 45. Look closely at verse 5. What does this teach us about unlikely circumstances?

_____

_____

_____

_____

_____

2) What boundaries would restrict God from meeting your needs?

_____

_____

_____

_____

_____

3) The Lord can give us four answers. He can say "Yes," he can say, "No," he can say, "Wait," and he can answer in a way that you don't expect. In what ways has the Lord met your needs (or the needs of those you are close to) by giving an answer you didn't expect?

_____

_____

_____

_____

_____

But seek first His kingdom and His
righteousness,
And all these things will be given
to you as well.
Therefore do not worry about
tomorrow, for
tomorrow will worry about itself.

Matthew 6:33 (NIV)

10
EVERY DAY IS A GIFT

In 2001 tragedy struck my family. My wife Teresa was diagnosed with glioblastoma multiforme (GBM), the most aggressive known form of brain cancer. She died two and a half years later at the age of 38. You might say that God doesn't perform miracles because tragedies such as this happen. Why can't He just perform a miracle and eliminate all disease? Well, there are no diseases in the presence of God. His Kingdom is heaven and we are not there yet.

For now we live in a fallen world where struggles are unavoidable. Yes, to our blessing we have his scriptures to guide us. The Bible is clear that *"all things work together for the good of those that love Him."* (Romans 8:28) I'm also reminded of the Old Testament story of Job where we read of a heavenly dialogue between Satan and God. Job was completely unaware of God's purpose for his suffering; however, Job's faithfulness through suffering was what brought glory to God! One of my favorite verses, Isaiah 55:8-9, also proves this—*"My ways are not your ways. My thoughts are not your thoughts. As far as the heavens are above the earth are my ways above your ways and my thoughts above your thoughts."* Yes, many things happen in our lives that we do not understand because of reasons that are only known in Heaven.

In my first book, *Help! I am a Christian. Why am I Sick?*, I wrote about why disease occurs from a spiritual point-of-view. I researched all the Bible stories where someone was touched by disease. There was a wide variety of occurrences. I then summarized the situations into seven categories. I invite you to read that book if you seek to better understand disease and its role in human life. I include many details of my personal experience in that book that are not included herein.

I believe that God approved the "trial" of disease for Teresa and our family. As humans we tend to view someone's homegoing from this earthly existence to our heavenly home as a bad or terribly sad event. However, from the Lord's viewpoint, a person's passing is not so. Also, I don't believe that someone's passing is a form of punishment. Sometimes it is an act of grace. It was my experience that, in the midst of tragedy, God poured out His grace upon Teresa, our entire family, and me.

My wife's health problem began with a migraine headache that lasted several days. She saw the doctor and was prescribed two medications but they didn't help. Finally, we went to the hospital so that an MRI could be performed of her head. The scan revealed a mass of cancer cells in the right frontal lobe of her brain. From the beginning doctors suspected that it was GBM just by its appearance. They confirmed their diagnosis with a biopsy while she was in surgery. Afterwards the doctors explained that 95 percent of GBM patients do not live more than 24 months. We also read of this horrendous illness on the Internet. Even for those persons who survive beyond two years, the overall survival rate is less than 2 percent. It is a relatively obscure form of cancer that affects approximately 20,000 people per year. The research for a cure is somewhat limited because of the relatively small number of cases.

There's no known cure for glioblastoma multiforme; however, some treatments will slow its growth for a limited time. The first treatment was a craniotomy (brain surgery). It's a traumatic experience to the brain and involves doctors shaving the patient's head, cutting and pulling back the scalp, then, with a specialized saw, opening the skull and temporarily removing the bone. At this point, with the brain exposed, doctors actually surgically cut away and remove the parts of the brain that are visibly affected by the cancer cells. Afterwards the bone is placed back into its place and held in position with screws. Then the surgeon pulls the scalp back into place and closes the incision with sutures.

The specific results of this surgery are unpredictable. However, side effects can be anticipated based on the area of the brain that's been operated on. I talked to the husband of one GBM patient. His wife had a probe inserted into her brain—not a full surgery—for the purpose of performing a biopsy. She went into surgery fully mobile and came out of the surgery paralyzed in all four limbs. Other consequences can be continued cranial pain and phantom pain, altered personality, partial to full paralysis, bleeding or swelling in the brain, blurred vision or blindness, loss of memory, and the loss of coordination and fine motor skills. This is not, however, a complete list.

Although it was difficult to receive the news that Teresa had the disease and such a bad prognosis, we were grateful that she went through surgery without consequence.

It was a huge relief to see that she was the same sweet and kind person after surgery as before. What were the chances of this happening after complex brain surgery? In the midst of the tragedy, we received an unexpected miracle in our ordinary lives.

The day Teresa left work because of that initial migraine was the last day she worked. After surgery she had a six-week recovery period followed by another six weeks of radiation treatments. Then she began a strenuous chemotherapy routine. We had the best of care and even traveled to Duke University in North Carolina to visit one of the few medical research facilities for GBM in our country. We followed the protocol of the doctors at Duke, and, because of the blessing of God, Teresa did not have a recurrence for more than two years.

Her diagnosis changed our lives permanently. As I reflect, I remember the dark cloud of dread and worry that never left, and the helpless feeling I had when the woman I loved was so terribly ill after receiving chemotherapy treatments. However, I also learned in a more intense way how each day was indeed a gift from God. Even when you're not terminally ill, each day is a gift. I've met widows and widowers whose loved one passed without warning. There was no chance to say good-bye or to gain closure as Teresa and I so richly enjoyed. In our situation we'd approach each day by, "hoping for the best but being prepared for the worst." Teresa even took her mother and our daughter on a trip to visit relatives. They stayed more than a week. Teresa also participated in a daytime Bible study with other women and spent quality time in God's Word. Yes, she truly made the most of each day.

God's Kingdom is not about accumulating material possessions. It's about our relationship with our Father in Heaven and His people. During those two years we met other GBM patients who were much worse than Teresa. And there were others who acquired the disease and died from it during the short time we knew them.

Unfortunately, the cancer returned just a month after the two-year mark and Teresa passed away five months later. Still, with all the incredible odds going against her she experienced two years of good health and quality life because the Lord extended His grace to her even in the midst of tragedy. I know the Lord intervened and gave us those two glorious years. I believe they were a special gift and an unexpected miracle in our ordinary lives.

DISCUSSION QUESTIONS:

1) Sometimes we think of a miracle as something that happens in an instant or is a one-time event. Consider the great amount of time the Hebrews spent in the wilderness. What sustaining miracles did they experience? (There were at least four. See Exodus chapters 13, 16, and 17.) What do sustaining miracles tell us about the character of God?

_____

_____

_____

_____

2) Read Genesis 32:22-32. What were the long-term results of Jacob's miraculous encounter with God? What purpose do you think it served?

_____

_____

_____

_____

3) When the scriptures say, "Don't worry about tomorrow," what do you think is an appropriate and biblical attitude to live by day-to-day?

_____

_____

_____

_____

But he who enters by the door is a shepherd of the sheep. To him the doorkeeper opens, and the sheep hear his voice, and he calls his own sheep by name and leads them out.

John 10:2-3 (NASV)

11
WORDS OF COMFORT

I was raised in a conservative denominational Christian church. When I was in the eighth grade our family left that church for an independent, nondenominational church. Both churches were places of strong biblical teaching; however, I'd never learned details of some spiritual topics, one of which I wish to share. This chapter relates a story of how the Lord clearly spoke to me and then how He later spoke to Teresa during the most difficult season of our lives.

Teresa was diagnosed with brain cancer in September. Living with the disease was difficult and it was equally as hard to live with the treatments because of their many side effects. Depending on the drug she was taking at the time, the side effects included nausea, vomiting, constipation, headaches, and body aches. And, she lost her hair, then grew it back, and she lost weight just to later gain it back.

Teresa was not a person to show much emotion; however, her illness affected our entire family. Nonetheless, we didn't like seeing her struggle. I recall a day when she received an intravenous treatment of chemotherapy in the doctor's office. On the way home, while driving on the busiest freeway in North Dallas, she started sweating profusely and then vomited unexpectedly in the truck. I pulled over onto the shoulder, and while cars and trucks whizzed by at 70 miles per hour, I cleaned her up with a towel. Then I drove her on home and put her to bed. It was three days later before she felt like moving around again.

That first year we traveled to her parents' home for Christmas. Their home was on a country road outside a small town in Oklahoma. It was a nice change of scenery and the kids were excited to see their cousins. The house was decorated for Christmas, everyone was excited to exchange gifts, and there was a spread of food that covered the kitchen. However, Teresa was scheduled to take the last dose of a chemo series that afternoon. So she waited until we arrived at her parents' before she took it. As expected, later that evening she began feeling badly. Her family knew this may happen, so they made plans for everyone to spend the night at her sister's house, leaving Teresa and me alone for the night.

Teresa was sick for several hours. I helped by getting towels and washing her face. We were in her parents' bedroom because it had easy access to the master bathroom. Finally, she was able to remain in bed and she fell asleep. It was well below freezing outside the house, but inside it was cozy and warm. The blankets on the bed were soft and inviting. We both slept peacefully until about 3 a.m. When I awakened it was absolutely quiet; there was no sound of wind, cars, or birds. It was the kind of quiet that makes your ears ring.

I remember listening to her breathing and then asking in a soft whisper, "Are you asleep?" She said, "No," so we snuggled up and enjoyed a very peaceful and loving moment. After a while I said, "Let me pray for you."

I had been memorizing verses on healing, so I sat up and put my hands on her and prayed aloud the verses that came to mind. As I prayed, I had what I called an interrupting thought inside my head. It was different from my normal thoughts because it was loud and not my voice. It was like when you are talking on the phone and your child walks up and begins talking and interrupting your conversation. You're hearing his voice and your voice at the same time. I could see from her body language that Teresa didn't hear it. I actually looked to see if someone were in the room, but there was no one. Then, I paused in silence and the inner voice spoke again. It said, "Klay, I'm calling Teresa home because it serves my purpose. I will take care of you." It was the first time an experience such as this had happened to me. I didn't know what to think so I kept it to myself.

About a month later I shared this with a mature Christian man and trusted friend. He told me that I had heard the voice of the Holy Spirit. Maybe so, I thought, but why would the Holy Spirit say that? You see, I was not ready to receive the words I heard. It took me two years before I could accept them. I just couldn't find peace with letting go of the woman whom I loved. I didn't share it with Teresa until later.

People will say, referring to my loss of Teresa, "I don't know how you were able to go through that." I tell them that God was merciful and gave me a personal word. As I look back over the years, it was that word which has resonated in my heart and still gives me great comfort. I know with confidence that Teresa's homegoing was neither an accident nor an oversight. I know that God did not punish her, but that He called her home because it served His purpose. I had received a gracious word from my merciful Lord and it was another unexpected miracle in my ordinary life.

The Lord's kindness wasn't extended only to me. He also touched Teresa one day. However, He did it quite differently. The disease had recurred in the twenty-fifth month. The cancer this time appeared on the MRI as a small white area about the size of a nickel and it was in a new location. It was ear level and more centrally located deep in the gray matter of the brain. There was no way to remove the mass surgically without severe consequences. Teresa declined to have a second surgery. The only treatment option was a final round of radiation.

The week after Teresa completed radiation, she had another MRI, whose results showed that there was no growth of the cancer cells. That particular morning she drove to the shopping mall and back home. When she walked in the door, she came to me with urgency and said, "Klay, I have to tell you something." She was clearly moved. While she was driving, she had an indescribable peace come over her. She said she felt "whole"—body, soul, and mind. As she told me this she wept. It was not her nature to show this much emotion, but it was a very significant moment to her. We hugged and she told me all the details. I believe Teresa was strongly compelled to share the specifics with me. Neither of us truly understood what it meant, but, I felt the Holy Spirit had specifically touched her. Only later was it that I made sense of it all and realized the big picture.

When I look back on that day, I see that it was the beginning of the end. It was her last good week. I think the Lord touched her to prepare her for the stressful months that were to come. He gave her a glimpse of what her life would be like in heaven. As the cancer grew, the first visible sign was paralysis in her left facial muscles. She could not offer her radiant smile. Then her left arm became paralyzed and unusable, and then her left leg. For the last two months of her life she needed a wheelchair to move around in our home.

Among the toughest moments in my life was after Teresa had received all the treatments possible and her doctor told us she didn't have anything else to try. Teresa responded, "I'll just trust the Lord from here." In other words, the doctor could no longer help us, yet Teresa yielded herself to receive what the Lord had approved for her. I hugged the doctor and told her thank you. I then wept as we left the doctor's office for the last time. Teresa was standing on her faith and she was filled with grace and love until the end of her life just a few short weeks later. I believe she had this peace because she knew the Lord was constantly with her, just as His Word says.

I recall the teaching of a Dallas Theological Seminary professor on how to understand when God moves. He said, "When God moves you can see His handprint." I think that is what was on display the day Teresa shared her feeling of wholeness—an aspect of the true character of God. I experienced the lovingkindness and grace of the Lord. It was a time when He intervened in Teresa's life and touched her so that she would be comforted. He loved her very much.

The words of comfort spoken to me and the indescribable feeling of peace given to Teresa were most definitely unexpected miracles in our ordinary lives.

DISCUSSION QUESTIONS:

1) Consider the "handprint" of God. What attributes of God's character may be seen as evidence of His intervention?

_____

_____

_____

_____

_____

2) Think of the many ways in which the Lord spoke to His people. Consider 1 Kings 19, Deuteronomy 5:1-27, Acts 9:1-9, and John 10:3. List as many others as you can.

_____

_____

_____

_____

_____

3) What are various ways the Lord may speak to you or direct you?

_____

_____

_____

_____

_____

*And my God will supply all your
needs according
to His riches in glory in Christ Jesus.*

Philippians 4:19 (NASV)

12

A DIVINE EXIT AND A NEW DIRECTION

Many generations ago, the Bible records, Jacob's family was granted favor from the Lord during a difficult time. In the midst of a long drought and after an amazing chain of events, Jacob, then called Israel, and his family received life-saving grain and shelter after traveling to Egypt. Then, after the drought ended Jacob and his descendants received a place to live in a fertile farming area. These descendants who were blessed through Jacob's son Joseph, however, didn't always find favor from the Egyptians.

Over time, an initial family of 70 grew to become a great nation of more than one million people. The Egyptian rulers, who at one time loved Joseph, had all died; thus, Joseph's many achievements were long forgotten. Through many generations spanning the next 400 years, conflict arose between the Hebrews and the Egyptians. The result? The Hebrews became enslaved to the Egyptians. In other words, a positive situation turned bad and, thus, the Hebrews cried out to God for freedom from oppression. I can certainly identify with the Hebrews.

In Exodus we read that Pharaoh refused to let the Hebrew people leave Egypt. Here's where we learn the story of Moses and the ten plagues. The plagues were a divine demonstration of power and displeasure designed to persuade Pharaoh to "let my people go" (in the words of a well-known spiritual). The Hebrews faced a constant battle with Pharaoh, begging him to allow them to depart Egypt. Finally, Pharaoh gave them freedom. Under the leadership of Moses, the Israelites headed into the wilderness, back to the land God had promised them.

While the Israelites camped in the wilderness, Pharaoh changed his mind again, for one final showdown. He mounted his chariot and commanded his well-trained and fully armed army—600 chariots strong—to assault the unarmed Hebrews in what would appear to be a bloody, vengeful route. Then (my favorite part), with the people backed up against the waters of the Red Sea, filled with fear, and having nowhere to go, Moses said, *"Do not be afraid. Stand firm and you will see the deliverance the Lord will bring you today. The Egyptians you see today you will never see again. The Lord will fight for you; you need only to be still."* (Exodus 14:13, NIV).

I relate to the Hebrew people in this passage because I had been toiling, over the course of four years, 50- to 60-hour work weeks at my oil change business. It wasn't a slave and master situation; however, I'd received no pay for all my efforts and I certainly felt oppressed. My wife was fighting a terminal illness and I simply didn't have the desire or energy to work any longer. I was physically exhausted and emotionally drained. So I decided it was time to sell the store and move on. It was my time to leave Egypt.

Selling a business is a complex process. You must find a buyer who is qualified for a large bank loan, capable of operating a retail business, and someone who has substantial cash for a down payment. It's common to have a sale contract fall through as a result of the many details that sometimes just do not work out. The ups and downs of the sales process remind me greatly of the ten plagues and how the pharaoh repeatedly changed his mind. These plagues taught many lessons, but mostly they revealed a "process" that demonstrated the character of God. The overall purpose? So that everyone would know the Great I Am!

God certainly could have made things simple and delivered the Hebrews in a matter of minutes and been done with it. But He did not do it that way because it wouldn't have fulfilled His purpose. His purpose for us, even today as in times of old, is that we live in a relationship with the Lord, guided by the Holy Spirit. We build our faith on the fact that we trust Him. Then, we are to give testimony to others for what God has done in our lives. Therefore, this process and the struggles that come with it bring growth in our faith and reliance on God. The Bible is very clear that without faith it is impossible to please God (Hebrews 11:6).

I spoke with many prospects in my sale "process" whom I viewed as similar to the Israelites who were caught up in the process taught by the plagues. Most persons who inquired were not qualified; and, I worked with one buyer more than four months only to have his contract fall through. The words of Moses resonate with me, *"Stand firm and you will see the deliverance the Lord will bring you today.... You need only to be still."* The New Living Translation relates it more succinctly with, *"Just stay calm."*

So, after a lengthy sale process, the Lord moved in my situation. A man with an identical store seven miles away offered to buy my store. He had all that was needed to be successful. The process with this buyer went without a hitch. The many details fell into place, the loan was approved, and within a few months the new owner took over the operations.

One reason that I am confident that the Lord intervened in my life regarding the sale of my business was the timing of my departure from this Egypt. The sale of the store occurred in late November, thus, I enjoyed the freedom to stay home and give my wife my undivided attention until her death four months later. Additionally, I was not in a healthy frame of mind to run the business after such a great personal loss.

A second reason that I am confident God had intervened in my life was because of the financial blessing of the sale. I didn't become financially independent for the rest of my life; however, I made a fair profit from the overall business investment. And, it seemed as if I finally received a huge stack of paychecks for all my hard work. The financial blessing allowed me to enjoy financial stability. I'm very grateful to the Lord for His hand of mercy during the sale of my business.

Sometimes when the Lord speaks it is without words. For example, the Bible contains a story of how Moses was on Mt. Sinai and there was thunder and lightning and the mountain trembled violently (Exodus 19:16-18). And, at the point of Jesus' death, when he gave up his spirit, the earth shook and the rocks split (Matthew 27:51). And, in Revelation, John speaks of how in the future there will be flashes of lightning, rumblings, peals of thunder and a severe earthquake (Revelation 16:18).

The sale of my business was not suspenseful nor did it come with flashing lights or any form of danger. It was a long process that resulted in both material blessings for me and the strengthening of my faith in God. It was a definitive turning point and a new direction in my life, and it felt as if my personal mountain trembled to remind me that the Lord was there. It was an unexpected miracle in my life, for the Lord certainly intervened.

DISCUSSION QUESTIONS

1) Survey 1 Samuel 6 through 2 Samuel 24. In what quiet and unexpected ways did the Lord intervene in the life of King David? How do you think these interventions changed King David's faith in and relationship with the Lord?

_____

_____

_____

2) Have you experienced any "processes" in your journey with the Lord? In what way have these experiences changed you and helped you grow your faith?

_____

_____

_____

3) At the age of 120, Moses was told by the Lord that he would not enter the Promised Land with the people he loved. Moses knew his life would end soon. As he reflected on his life, his last words to the people were, "Be strong and courageous. Do not be afraid or terrified because of them, for the LORD your God goes with you; He will never leave you nor forsake you." (Deut 31:6). As you reflect on your life what parting words would you leave your loved ones?

_____

_____

_____

❧

*Surely goodness and lovingkindness will
follow me all the days of
my life, and I will
dwell in the house of the Lord forever.*

Psalm 23:6 (NASV)

❧

13

ONLY ONE SET OF FOOTPRINTS IN THE SAND?

A famous poem called "Footprints in the Sand," by Mary Stevenson, relates the story of a person who is walking on the beach with the Lord. Two sets of footprints are visible in the sand for most of the journey. Then, during the lowest and saddest times of the journey, the speaker says that the trail has only one set of footprints. The person asks the Lord why he had been left alone. After all, the Lord had promised to always be with him. The Lord's answer? The single set of footprints was not a time when the Lord left; but, rather, was a time when He was carrying the person. This chapter represents a time in my life when the Lord carried me.

My mother had not felt well for more than a year. An auto accident had left her with a bruised torso and two broken toes. She thought her poor health was a lingering result of the accident. She finally underwent medical testing, and, in April, the doctor told her she had cancerous lesions on her liver. She had six months to live without treatments and perhaps a year and a half with aggressive chemotherapy and radiation treatments. She and my father chose a course of treatment that they felt would give her the best chance of survival and the best quality of life. It was all to no avail. She passed away the Monday following Thanksgiving Day, just seven months after her diagnosis.

The homegoing of a loved one can be the lowest and saddest time in someone's life. It's nearly impossible to stay clear-headed and hopeful while you watch as your loved one loses his or her health. Oftentimes, there's a broken heart that goes with the disease, because, with the advancing illness, life's dreams fade and hope is lost. The pending separation brings unwanted changes for caregivers and friends. They all hurt for their loved one who is suffering.

I sat with my mother many times during her illness and I comforted her as best I could. I was never certain during that time whether the Lord would take her home or allow her health to be restored. But I remember the feeling of dread I had when my grandparents were ill and near death. I hated the mere thought of my father calling me in the middle of the night to tell me that my mother had died. I hated the idea of driving down the long dark road to his house and then finding him alone with her breathless body still in their bed. I prayed that such a situation would not occur. I asked the Lord to be merciful and to extend His lovingkindness during my mother's last days.

The Lord heard my prayers. My mother passed rather quickly. She felt good enough to enjoy Thanksgiving dinner with her brother and two sisters. The following Sunday she had significant pain and she slept most of the day. The next day, Monday, her best friend of more than forty years had already made plans to stay with her the entire day. They always enjoyed each other and just her presence and her voice brought comfort. That Monday morning the hospice nurse came to check on my mother after the painful Sunday. She then asked to speak with me and my father and told us that my mother's body was showing all the signs of shutting down. She told us that my mother would probably not live more than two or three days. My mother did not live that long. She passed away that day at four o'clock in the afternoon.

When I look back on that time I can see clearly how the Lord poured out His grace and mercy on us all. There was no midnight phone call or long drive in the dark. My mother did not linger in pain and she spent her last day on this earth with her best friend, my father, and me. I believe the Lord is very sensitive to these prayers and is quick to respond. I believe we all experienced an unexpected miracle when the Lord intervened in our lives that day.

Similar things happened when my wife passed away five and a half years later. It's most common for brain cancer patients to simply sleep more and more until they lapse into a coma. If there is pain the doctors provide medication to make the person comfortable. We had known of another brain cancer patient who lingered in a coma for fourteen days. I did not want the same for Teresa. In one of our heart-to-heart talks long before her passing, I told Teresa not to stay on this earth any longer than necessary. I told her to go with the first angel who showed up to escort her to heaven.

On Friday morning March 12, I helped Teresa to the bathroom at 8 a.m. When I put her back to bed she hugged me and told me she loved me. She was a kindhearted person and those were the last words she spoke to me. The hospice nurse arrived at 10 a.m. to check on her and for the first time Teresa was nonresponsive. The nurse told us she had slipped into a coma and that it could potentially last a while, possibly three to five days.

I don't remember who was at the house that day; people came and went all day. I was very tired and we rotated sitting with Teresa. That night I slept in my son's room and I went to bed early because I knew that I would be needed in the early morning hours. I knew

Teresa's mother wanted to lie on the bed beside her, which was a good idea because it would allow her mother the time she needed to be alone with her daughter. Additionally, Teresa's sister felt a strong prompting to leave her house and drive to our home. She lived four and a half hours away, so she left at 8 p.m. that evening and arrived at our house a little after midnight.

Shortly after midnight they awakened me and said that Teresa was struggling to breathe. It was time for Teresa to go home. I was grateful that she did not linger three to five days. She passed away at approximately 1:30 a.m. We were all with her when the angels arrived for her glorious departure.

That was a second time that the Lord poured out His love and kindness. Everyone in the room had a broken heart but we all had closure and peace. It was not a time or a feeling that we as humans can orchestrate. For Teresa, the Lord's goodness and lovingkindness followed her all the days of her life and then she went to dwell in the House of the Lord forever. For the rest of us, it was like the Footprints in the Sand poem. There was just one set of footprints in the sand that night. Truly the Lord was carrying us.

Through this gracious homegoing of my beloved wife, I experienced another unexpected miracle in my ordinary life.

DISCUSSION QUESTIONS

1) The Lord's character is absolute and cannot change. What character traits of His are displayed in the story above?

_____

_____

_____

_____

2) In the New Living Translation John 1:16 reads, _"From His abundance we have all received one gracious blessing after another."_ Read this verse in other Bible translations to understand the full meaning of the phrase. How does the meaning of "One gracious blessing after another" apply to your life?

_____

_____

_____

_____

3) Why do you think the Lord allows us to suffer? Knowing that we do suffer, what conclusion can we make about our time here on this earth?

_____

_____

_____

_____

. . . the kingdom of heaven is like a merchant seeking fine pearls, and upon finding one pearl of great value, he went and sold all that he had and bought it.

Matthew 13:44-46 (NASV)

14
WRITING A MUSICAL COMEDY

I work full-time as a certified public accountant. Accounting has been my career for almost 30 years. However, by an unexpected series of events, I've co-authored a Broadway-style musical comedy with my brother, Brent. It's called Oil Change the Musical Comedy.

So what's so miraculous about that? Well, the way it all came to be is what's so miraculous. I never once sat down and decided that I would write a musical comedy because a project such as that is very overwhelming and I have no formal training. Writing more than two hours of theatrical presentation including eighteen original songs? No, I certainly can't do that. I'm an accountant! But, I did! I just couldn't see the big picture at the time I began down this exciting road.

I mentioned earlier how the Lord spoke words of comfort to me during my wife's illness. He said, "I will take care of you." This statement could have meant various things—it's only now, many years later, that I can see some aspects of His promise to me. What I believe He meant was that my life would go in a new direction. I would do things that were completely different from when I was married and He would guide me down new paths.

The first two years after my wife's passing were difficult. I had many weeks of feeling depressed and hopeless. This is normal considering the loss I had been through, but the biggest challenge was working. I didn't feel motivated. I was no longer goal-oriented.

The plans I'd made for my life were gone and setting new goals seemed pointless. So for the first time in my life I did something different. I listened to my creative promptings and I took the time to truly enjoy a newfound and unexplored interest.

My creative interests are in writing lyrics to songs and telling funny stories. I actually wrote lyrics to a song for my wife, Teresa. My brother, Brent, is a gifted musician and music producer who put the lyrics to music and recorded the song. I was quite pleased with the results. I gave Teresa the song four months before she died. She loved it and played it for everyone. I thought it was fulfilling to write the lyrics to a song and then hear them put to music. So I became motivated to write more.

I'm a country music fan and my favorite artist is Brad Paisley. I particularly like his humorous songs so I used them as a guide to develop my songs. I had multiple song ideas that resulted from operating an oil change business for five years! So I followed Brad's song structure and began putting pen to paper.

There was one set of lyrics, then two, then another. I'd send them to my brother and he'd write the music. He could see that I was having fun and he was ready for us to be a team. We wrote eight songs the first year. Without a doubt it was fun, but it was not something I took seriously. I had no ambition to ever have my songs published. Possibly, I thought, I could learn to play the guitar and sing the songs myself, an idea I have since abandoned, but songwriting was really no more than a hobby.

One day Brent sent me a recently produced recording of a song he'd composed with lyrics I'd written. It was a funny song about a redneck guy chasing a girl, not because the guy liked the girl, but because he wanted to drive her truck. I played the song for friends at church. One friend said his high school buddy played trumpet for a top country star. He offered to send the song to his friend and he guaranteed the country star would hear it. Well, it was fun to dream about such a possibility and it was a nice compliment, but the thought of someone other than my brother singing that song was not appealing to me, so I passed on the offer. However, the offer did indeed plant a seed and I began to think how it may be exciting if all the songs I'd co-written with my brother were somehow published together.

Then it occurred to me that most of the song lyrics that I'd written were connected to the oil change business I had owned, and the idea occurred to me that these songs could be developed into a musical comedy about daily life at an oil change business. I had loved musical comedies since high school and I attended a school that produced some hilarious shows over the years. The high school teacher-director was excellent and we had many talented students. Also during my teen years, I was fortunate to see many professionally produced shows. So from the seeds planted by that teacher and the professional productions that enamored me, I decided to combine my songs into a musical comedy. I began to envision what such a musical might look like on stage.

My next step was to find a professional writer. I went to a writers' group, asked a college professor for advice, and searched the internet. I spoke to a few writers, but made my decision after talking to the director of a theater. We talked until he understood what I had in mind. He said that my ideas were quite specific and that I should just write the script myself! He referred me to a book that gave guidance on script formatting and he offered to review my work. I had my answer, so I started writing my first script. I viewed it as an exciting adventure.

I didn't know it at the time but I've come to understand that creating a musical is a lengthy process. Writing the script, writing and producing the music (sheet music included), and preparing the musical for a premier production is usually a ten-year process. The most connected and talented people can reduce that time frame to three to five years, but that's also with significant financial backing.

One reason the process takes so long is that a show is "workshopped" on multiple levels before it is considered for full production. A workshop is held so that actors can present different versions of the script and then the reviewing audience provides feedback for the purpose of improving the musical. For example, the 1976 Tony Award winning musical, *A Chorus Line,* was workshopped more than 10 times before it became such a popular show.

Shows are first workshopped for the script, then for blocking, then for the music, and then the choreography. Large commercial productions test run for two or three weeks before their official opening night. One of today's most popular musical productions, *Wicked,* was written and produced in San Francisco and then rewritten before it was moved to Broadway almost a year later. Only after opening night is the script "frozen" and no more changes are made.

With a completed script and music in hand, I sought to have *Oil Change the Musical Comedy* workshopped. I had trouble arranging a workshop in my city, so I put an ad in the Manhattan edition of Craigslist. I advertised, "Out-of-state playwright seeks assistance from experienced director to conduct a workshop for a new musical." I received five responses. One was from a lady who owned a small repertory company. We talked on the phone and seemed to have a great rapport, so we set a date. Off I went to New York City for a week in the theater business! That first workshop was fascinating, fun, and very productive. It led to many script and music revisions. We held a second workshop that led to even more revisions, then there was a third and a fourth!

Only God knows what the future holds and certainly no guarantees exist that *Oil Change the Musical Comedy* will ever be produced. However, it has a very positive outlook and it's taken on a life of its own. If it all ended today I would be grateful for how the whole experience has blessed me and changed me as a person. Not only has it been a fulfilling project for me, but, it's brought newness to my life.

One of the biggest changes in me is that I've learned to enjoy life's journey in a more skillful way. I've learned how the Lord shares His creativity with me, but at the same time, He doesn't show me the big picture all at once. He shows me things one day at a time. I've learned to receive His leading by writing down my thoughts and ideas and then later assembling them piece by piece. After I'd completed the musical I was able to see that God was actually giving me something bigger, I just didn't know it at the time. When I look back, I see an impressive body of work that was orchestrated way beyond my own feeble abilities. The script is funny and family-friendly, and, combined with my brother's excellent musical composition, it's an overall good production.

I don't think this musical chapter is finished. I hope it will go on for years to come and that I can write more stories about *Oil Change the Musical Comedy* and other creative experiences. For now, I know emphatically that the Lord has unfolded a new chapter in my life. He's given me the gift of a musical comedy, but it is more than that. It is a gift of experiencing Him day-by-day. Truly, through this new creative process I've experienced another unexpected miracle in my ordinary life.

DISCUSSION QUESTIONS

1) You will hear it said that "the end justifies the means." This is said by "destination minded" people. Other people say, "Enjoy the journey" or "Stop and smell the roses." What mindset do you think better reflects the mind of the Lord? What Bible verses or stories can you tell that support your answer?

_____

_____

_____

2) When we consider the creativity of our Father and knowing that we are made in His image, what does this say about us as creative beings?

_____

_____

_____

3) In the Amplified Bible, Ephesians 1:17 reads, *"[17] [For I always pray to] the God of our Lord Jesus Christ, the Father of glory, that He may grant you a spirit of wisdom and revelation [of insight into mysteries and secrets] in the [deep and intimate] knowledge of Him."* Considering that life is a journey (question 1) and that we are creative and made in the image of a creative God (question 2), how does the broader meaning of this verse affect our daily fellowship with Him?

_____

_____

_____

*Because of the Lord's great
love we are not
consumed, for His compassions
never fail.
They are new every morning; great is
your faithfulness.*

Lamentations 3:22-23 (NIV)

15
A FIERY FURNACE THAT FAILED TO IGNITE

I've lived in the same house for many years. It's a nice house and I'm very blessed, but it also means that I've had to change or repair many things over the years. Several years ago it was the water heater. My house has two water heaters—one in the attic, which services the bathrooms and one in the garage, which services the kitchen and laundry room.

Water heaters have an eight- to ten-year lifespan. So as Murphy's Law would have it, after we'd lived in our home almost eight years, the attic water heater quit working. I try to be Handyman Hank, but I remember thinking how difficult the water heater would be for me to replace with my limited skills. So I called the plumber to come to our rescue. He repaired it, but the company charged me a fortune! I was thrilled to once again have warm water, even as I lamented about the expense!

Then about five years ago the water heater in the garage went out. So instead of calling the plumber, I went to the home improvement store to purchase the materials to repair it myself and save some money! I spoke with a knowledgeable employee in the plumbing department and explained what I wanted. He said that I could repair the water heater and he even showed me how! My biggest concern was going to be the pipe welding. I'd never learned how to weld. But he explained that there are flex hoses and special connectors made so that true, old-fashioned welding was no longer necessary. It looked like a rather straightforward job, so away I went. A new drip pan, a new vent pipe, a new overflow hose, and new flex hoses for everything else. In a matter of a few hours, the new water heater was working great and I was pleased with the amount of money I'd invested to repair it and the money I'd saved.

A few more years passed and the water heater in the attic needed to be replaced for the second time. So I decided to change it out just as I'd done with the one in the garage. I thought it would be more difficult, but only because removing the defective heater meant it had to be hauled down the small folding staircase that led from the attic to the floor below and then the new water heater had to be lifted up the small staircase and positioned into place.

So, I recruited my two sons to do the muscle work! With three able-bodied men, the process was relatively quick. Once the water heater was in place it was actually easier to install than the one located in the garage because the attic was more spacious than the small garage closet. In a few hours the new hoses were on, the new gas line attached, and the overflow pipes and vents were working fine. We had warm water again. To be on the safe side I checked it the next day and the following weekend to see if leaks had sprung or if anything else seemed unusual. Everything looked fine. Mission accomplished!

I replaced the water heater in September and in November we had our first cold spell. It was time to turn on the furnace. I turned the thermostat to heat but to my dismay it did not work. I thought, "Great, another repair bill." The furnace and the water heater are up the same staircase and they share the same attic area. So up the stairs I went again. One look at the furnace and I knew I could not repair it. So the next morning I called a repairman.

The heater specialist arrived later that day and quickly determined that the problem was the primary circuit board of the furnace. It was just too old to work anymore. But he also noticed a faint smell of gas. When he mentioned it I noticed it too, but I thought that it was a normal occurrence when a heater doesn't light. After all, it was a gas furnace. However, he disagreed. He said I should not smell gas at all. So he went to his truck and got his gas-sensing tool and returned to determine the source of the odor.

I learned something new that day. I learned that the gas used in our homes is actually heavier than air; it falls and accumulates near the floor instead of rising and dispersing upward as other gases do. Both my water heater and furnace are gas powered. The water heater is on a pedestal in the attic about three and a half feet high. The furnace is suspended from ceiling rafters. Below the furnace is an open space about three feet deep. When the serviceman pointed his gas sensor upward there was no response; when he pointed it downward, the alarm went off and left no doubt about the source of the odor. There was a large accumulation of gas in the three-foot space below the furnace! It was indeed a dangerous situation. When the repairman looked further, he found that the gas leak had nothing to do with the furnace. It was actually coming from the water heater that I'd replaced two months earlier!

When I had attached the gas line to the new water heater I used a coupling purchased from the home improvement store. I had also sealed it with white Teflon tape. The coupling was the correct size and had the correct threading, but what I didn't know is that the coupling was a compression coupling made with a beveled end. It was made to seal when it was under pressure. I did not need this type of coupling; I'd needed a standard quarter-inch coupling with no bevel. In addition, it would have made a better seal if I had used pipe putty and *not* tape! This difference was enough to allow a small pinhole leak of gas from the line where it was connected to the water heater.

If the pinhole leak had remained unabated, the gas accumulation would have grown in my attic. When it reached a height of four feet it would have been at the level of the flames in the furnace, *and* it would have ignited! An enormous explosion in my attic would have destroyed my home and could have even been fatal. The timing of the failing furnace was absolutely perfect.

To this day I am still amazed at how the Lord protected me. I am most grateful to the Lord for my furnace failing. I thank Him for His lovingkindness that *never* fails and His protection for my family and me! Once again, God was watching over me, and, for yet another time, I experienced an unexpected miracle in my ordinary life.

DISCUSSION QUESTIONS

1) Read Isaiah 54:17 and Matthew 6:26. What do these verses communicate about the Lord's desire to protect us?

_____

_____

_____

_____

_____

2) Read Lamentations 3:22-23 (quoted at the beginning of this chapter). How frequently does the Lord keep us from being consumed and how frequently do we receive His compassion?

_____

_____

_____

_____

_____

3) What are times in your life or your family's life that the Lord has extended you compassion, mercy, and protection?

_____

_____

_____

_____

_____

But thou art holy, O thou that inhabits the praises of Israel.

Psalm 22:3 (KJV)

16
WHAT'S ON YOUR LIST?

The unexpected miracles included herein are certainly not the only times I've felt the Lord intervening to protect me or direct me. Numerous other times the Lord has answered a prayer or affirmed me in a certain way.

When I graduated from the University of Texas with my accounting degree, I wasn't quite sure of what I wanted to do or where I would best fit into the workforce. Then the Lord opened a door that was unmistakable. I had worked part-time for a large printing company during my college years—a job I landed because the company owner was a family friend. This owner recommended me to an accounting firm that audited his financial statements. In addition, the audit manager of that firm was the brother-in-law of a classmate and friend. My friend made a recommendation too. Two separate connections with the same firm and I was hired. It was a good place for me to begin my accounting career and I was grateful to the Lord for preparing such a place specifically for me.

Chapter 14 tells the story of how *Oil Change the Musical Comedy* came to be. There was a time when I had conceived the idea but wasn't quite sure if I should pursue it. But, God certainly affirmed this idea. This incredible affirmation occurred while I was taking my children to meet up with their cousins for a visit in another state. Their cousins lived four and a half hours away, so a relative would agree to meet us in a town halfway.

On this particular trip, we met up with the kids' aunt and uncle. We'd stopped at a fast food restaurant to stretch our legs and enjoy a short visit. During the visit I shared with the relatives of my idea to compose a musical comedy. They listened intently and encouraged me. They already knew of the song I had written to Teresa. I shared with them my vision of how Teresa's song could be sung on a dark stage with a ballerina who was dancing in a lovely white dress. They agreed that it would be very beautiful. Then we walked to the car to leave. While standing to say good-bye, my brother-in-law looked down. There, lying on the ground was a toy ballerina about two inches tall. Obviously a child had dropped it on the pavement. My brother-in-law picked it up and said, "Here's your ballerina!" Then he handed it to me. I thought about it on the drive home. What are the chances of such a coincidence occurring? I said, "Thank you, Lord, for that affirmation. Yes, I will pursue this musical comedy idea."

I've had numerous other blessings. I live near a 400-acre park where I go frequently to escape the responsibilities and worries of daily life. I enjoy the wildlife that survives there in the shadow of urban sprawl. I've seen rabbits, beautiful predatory birds, a bobcat, raccoons, skunks, armadillos, and many snakes. One snake was a vibrant bright green tree snake about two feet long. It was beautiful and most eager to hide. I've found a couple of large turtles and one morning came upon a newborn turtle barely larger than a quarter. He was a trooper and determined to get away from me. I carried him to a less populated area of the park and released him.

I've also encountered a chameleon perched boldly on the sidewalk. Perhaps he thought he was invisible, but his red throat wouldn't allow him to go unnoticed. So I urged him to find a place where another person or a hungry hawk would not find him. He sprinted off running bow-legged into the field barely bending the blades of grass on which he ran. And finally, I was there after sundown on a warm summer evening. I was silently conversing with the Lord when I saw a wonderful shooting star roll across the sky just overhead. It broke into four dazzling strands as it disintegrated in the atmosphere. Wow! Just amazing!

Skeptics may say these are common occurrences. And I agree. I'm not the only one to see the rabbits, the baby turtle, or the chameleon. The shooting star would have happened even if I hadn't been witnessing it. Yet I believe the Lord reveals himself in common occurrences such as this every day. My situation is different merely because I was *paying attention.* How many times have we not seen the miracles of God in our lives merely because we do not choose to pay attention?

We know of the miracles that happened to the Hebrew nation because these events are recorded in the Old Testament. And I've listed my personal miracles in this book. Now I wish to challenge you.

Take a moment and count the miracles that you've experienced in your life. They can be life-changing events or they can be small things such as the ones I've recorded in this chapter. Either way, I challenge you to write them down. Print out your list and tape it to your refrigerator door, mirror, or computer monitor; or, place it in your Bible or journal. Then, from time to time, thank the Lord for all that He has done for you. Make your list visible so others will ask what it's all about. Give verbal testimony of how God has intervened in your life. Tell the stories to your children and even grandchildren. You'll both be encouraged and grow in faith.

As you tell the stories of the Lord's interventions in your life, you'll bring honor to the Lord. May it never be that we fail to see a miracle or fail to thank Him because we aren't paying attention! Just imagine—you can have your own personal version of the celebrative festivals the Jewish nation held in honor of the Lord's miracles.

If you've never known the Lord nor had Him in your life then please know this: With His whole essence He loves you and He wants to share each day with you. He promises in the Holy Bible to be with us and never leave us. He sent his Holy Spirit to be our helper and our guide. And He is never too busy to spend time with you. When you seek Him He will reveal Himself to you. There is just one requirement. You must believe that He exists (this is called faith) and believe that through His own perfect plan He removed all the barriers that keep us from knowing Him. He made our relationship possible through the sacrificial death of His son, the Messiah Savior Jesus Christ. Receive and believe these things and you will experience the Lord's involvement in your life. If you have never prayed to God then you might start with this prayer of faith.

> "Dear Heavenly Father, I believe in you and I understand that through your son Jesus Christ I may experience your presence in my life. I receive Jesus as my Savior and I ask you to indwell in my life from this day forward, Amen."

If you've prayed that prayer then I encourage you to pray as you go about your day everyday. I encourage you to read his Holy Bible and I encourage you to meet with other believers. Your faith will grow if you do these things. Experiencing God is the journey of a lifetime!

Start your list today.

How God has intervened, protected and directed my life.
My List of Miracles:

1)

2)

3)

4)

5)

Also, I encourage you to share your miracles with me and others on my website, www.GodsUnexpectedMiracles.com

ABOUT THE AUTHOR

Klay Rogers has served in lay ministries for over 30 years including church youth worker and leader, Young Life leader and in adult teaching ministries. His first book, *Help! I am a Christian. Why and I Sick?* is available on Amazon.com or from the author. He continues to volunteer his time as a speaker and guest teacher to further God's kingdom.

Klay holds a business degree from the University of Texas and has studied at Dallas Theological Seminary. He has worked for over 30 years professionally as a Certified Public Accountant in the Dallas, Texas area.

Klay can be contacted through the website, www. GodsUnexpectedMiracles.com, directly via e-mail at Klaycpa@ msn.com, or through Facebook.com.